true friend

A

take up & READ

PUBLICATION

Editorial Director: Elizabeth Foss
Copy Editors: Emily DeArdo and Rosie Hill
Illustration, Cover Art, & Calligraphy: Kristin Foss
Research & Development: Elizabeth Foss, Emily DeArdo, and Colleen Mitchell

Copyright © 2018 Take Up and Read

ISBN-13: 978-1720914624
ISBN-10: 1720914621

Scripture quotations are from New Revised Standard Version Bible: Catholic Edition, copyright © 1989, 1993 National Council of the Churches of Christ in the United States of America. Used by permission. All rights reserved worldwide.

take up & READ
COMMUNITY

VISIT US
takeupandread.org

BE SOCIAL
Facebook @takeupandread
Instagram @takeupandread
Twitter @totakeupandread

SEND A NOTE
totakeupandread@gmail.com

CONNECT
#TakeUpAndRead
#TrueFriendStudy

intro

Love one another as I have loved you.
John 13:34

True friendships are both historic and unconditional. Two or more people meet, and then, in the blink of an eye, they're looking back on decades of friendship, support, and above all, love.

When designing this book, I wanted to encourage intimate community while celebrating the seasonal colors of a summer release. Influences of bold, vivid color are found all over my studio in Connecticut. The hues have been seen before, picked up from people we've loved and places where we've lived and traveled. Most are influences of very close true friends.

Stark black sketches against bright white are inspired by Nicole, a lover of art deco and a classic black silhouette who lives in D.C. Bold red reminds me of Courtney's lipstick. Courtney is a poet, a thinker, and a casual deep conversationalist in San Francisco. Sap green is Rachel's color of choice to wear on nights out. Rachel, who lives in Vermont, is a passionate advocate for human rights and justice. Muted cadmium yellow and cobalt blue are colors I will always associate with Los Angeles and Erica, a fellow artist-heart with a deep love for people, travel, and taking the edge off of, well, my life's chaos. Deep earth tones remind me of my mother and the coastal Virginia town where I grew up: unconditional love and the most authentically organic life I've ever known. Serene greens and blues will always make me think of my mother-in-law who has a heart pacing for peace, grace, and the welcome of home. She has guided our whole team to create this book for you.

These people and colors almost always find themselves on my palette. These colors define friendship, and together they are harmonious, a complete masterpiece. I tend to use pure pigments directly on paper, mixing two colors at most at a time. Then I add more pigment, blending one at a time, always beginning with the true pigment.

Each of us comes to the table covered in the pigment of our own lives. Jesus holds the brush as he mixes our pigments together. We feel his presence, and together, we mix to create bold colors and values that create a masterpiece.

The colors of *True Friend* take us to an intimate global retreat, a celebration with our Lord, to stories of love, of bold color, and truth. Warm climates, fanned palms, humid backyards framed in dark green foliage, and picnic tables covered in vintage tablecloths influenced the interior artwork.

The simplest way to love one another is to open our hearts to friendship. There is no better guide for friendship and our calling to be true friends than the Bible. Friendship is everlasting, bold, and true. True friends can be closer than kin, closer than bonds of blood, knowledgeable of the intimate details of heirlooms, whether physical china tea cups hidden in the cupboard or the stories locked up tight in your heart.

Like a well-made ceramic vase, or a cherished porcelain tea cup, true friendships are wrapped up with care and kept close to us, wherever life leads us. These items make the cut when we have to pack up and move, as do our cherished friendships. The stories of the women who support us, shape us, and love us last longer than our most cherished heirlooms.

As you read the word, and listen to our stories and lessons, take out your pen and move with the inspiration of the true artist, our Lord. Take action with the word. Pray for the masterpiece. Live out your friendships boldly and vividly.

And may he transform you into a true friend.

Kristin Foss, Artist + Illustrator

intentional design

Each of our studies is created with unique, intentional design. We want to connect you with the Word and keep you connected throughout the day. In this Scripture study, we provided scholarly research to guide you through the ancient practice of **lectio divina** ("holy reading"). For detailed guidance on lectio divina, please see page 146. Fresh layouts, font design, and original artwork ensure that you have the tools to keep Him close to your heart, every day.

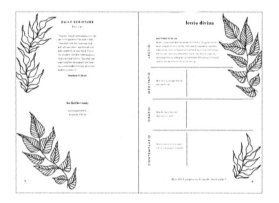

DAILY SCRIPTURE READING

This Scripture study includes daily Scripture readings. Notations for further reading are provided so you can open your Bible and further explore the Word.

LECTIO DIVINA

Reflect upon the Word and make a deep connection with your daily life.

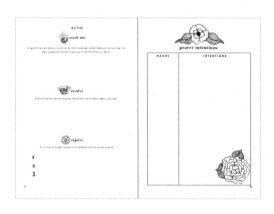

ACTIO

Follow the action plan with Reach Out, Resolve, and Rejoice.

PRAY FOR A FRIEND

Each day, we encourage you to write down the prayer intentions of your true friend(s).

WEEKLY SCRIPTURE VERSE

In this book, we will work on memorizing one key verse to reflect each week.

SELAH

Here is a chance to pause for prayer, praise, and rest.

At Take Up & Read, we want you to discover what prompts and pages are most useful to you. There is no perfect way to perform lectio—the important thing is that you take the time to have a conversation with God, using his Word as your guide.

journaling in action

LECTIO

2 Timothy 3:16-17
Written by St. Paul from prison to St. Timothy, who was in Ephesus. "All scripture" means all of the Old Testament but also maybe some of the Gospel accounts that became part of the New Testament.

MEDITATIO

What personal message does the text have for me?

The social media feeds I choose can compete with the message of the gospel. Scripture can be trusted. It should be my go-to when preparing for everything, my inspiration more than the internet.

ORATIO

What do I say to the Lord in response to His word?

Thank you for giving for giving me your Word. Remind me throughout my day, when I lose my way and look to other sources of direction, that You have everything I need to do Your good work.

CONTEMPLATIO

What conversion of mind, heart, and life is He asking of me today?

I think God is reminding me to get the ratio right: consult Scripture more than other things that compete for my time and attention.

How did I progress in living the Word today?

scripture
MEMORY
week one
day one

We spend so much time making lists, making plans, and engraving our to-dos in our planners and on our minds. What if we were intentional about hiding God's word deep in our hearts where it would speak us at all times? What if we always let God have the first word?

When we engrave the gospel into our minds, our hearts really know him. And what we know by heart can calm and encourage and sanctify our souls.

We cannot claim to know Christ without committing to knowing the word. He is the Word.

Repeating Scripture is how we breathe life into our faith at any moment, on any day (or in the middle of the night when life feels especially dark). Let memorizing Scripture—tucking it deep into your being—be a discipline of your daily life. Let it be what you do every day, beginning today. We promise it will change everything.

This week, we memorize a key verse from this study, the one from which we took our title.

• • • •

*Some friends play at friendship
but a true friend sticks closer than one's nearest kin.*

PROVERBS 18:24

Some friends play at friendship, but a true friend sticks closer than one's nearest kin.

PROVERBS 18:24

DAILY SCRIPTURE
day two

"Teacher, which commandment in the law is the greatest?" He said to him, "'You shall love the Lord your God with all your heart, and with all your soul, and with all your mind.' This is the greatest and first commandment. And a second is like it: 'You shall love your neighbor as yourself.' On these two commandments hang all the law and the prophets."

Matthew 22:36-40

for further study

Ecclesiastes 4:9-12
Proverbs 27:17-19

lectio divina

LECTIO

MATTHEW 22:36-40

Written by the apostle Matthew between 50-100 A.D., this Gospel was well-known in the early Church, and the most suited for catechetical instruction. In today's verses, known as the great commandment, Jesus shows the Pharisees that the most important commandment involves love, which animates the observance of the law and the Ten Commandments. Without love of God and neighbor, the rest of the law has no true meaning.

MEDITATIO

What personal message does the text have for me?

ORATIO

What do I say to the Lord in response to his word?

CONTEMPLATIO

What conversion of mind, heart, and life is he asking of me today?

How did I progress in living the word today?

I'm sitting at my father's kitchen table as I write today, and I can't help but be bemused. I grew up in a military family. I went to six different schools between the first and ninth grades. I was always the new girl. My dad sensed my loneliness; I think he understood it as best he could. He'd offer help and make suggestions and try to shore up my feeble, awkward attempts to make friends. Always, there was this agenda item: make friends.

And here I sit, all these years later, digging deeply into what Scripture says about making friends and thinking that my dad was close, but didn't quite get it right. My father's go-to advice was always the same.

"Go up to someone who looks nice and just say, 'Hi, my name's Elizabeth. Will you be my friend?'"

I never, ever did that. A very shy introvert who had read the dialogue between friends in Avonlea and on the banks of Plum Creek and who was holding out for kindred spirits, I was skeptical that anyone in the halls of my schools would think these were good opening lines. Truthfully, I was certain they'd be the prelude to bullying.

My father isn't here at this table today. He's in a memory care facility a few miles away. I want so much to talk with him about what we've learned writing this book. I want to tell him that he wasn't far off, but that the whole endeavor to make friends might have gone better if instead I'd focused on being a friend. Further, though he knew my tender heart well, I think that maybe he missed the mark when he advised how to choose the person who was to receive my plea for friendship.

What if he'd told Empathetic Elizabeth to look for the lonely and to offer to be a friend? What if, instead of seeking to fill a hole in me, I sought to see and to pour into the hole in someone else? I don't think this concept is too complex even for children. And I think that my dad would agree, if only we could have that conversation. I think that if I could tell him about the Scripture in these pages and God's plan for friendship, he'd be as enthused as I am today.

I think he'd hop right up and look for the opportunities still out there to be a good friend. I think he'd be really excited about God's call to befriend one another as he befriends us, and to be the friend that we want to have. I think he'd be excited to look back on his life and see that that is exactly where the best friendships had formed. I think we'd enjoy that "aha" moment together. I think my dad would heartily concur that the best friendship strategy is living out the commandment to love someone the way you want to be loved.

It has been a privilege and a joy to write this book with women who are my friends in the truest sense of the word. In some cases, we've poured into one another at the tenderest moments of a woman's life: moments of birth, of death, of loss, of astonishing joy. Those women are the reason I wasn't surprised when the Holy Spirit suggested that the girl who couldn't put three sentences together to make a friend all those years ago might try to create a book like this. Those women have shown me that when I seek to be a friend—to hear what he calls us to be in his name in someone else's life—I find a friend, I make a friend, I live in the freedom and joy of holy, faithful friendship.

Today, I'll tell my dad all about those friends and about the hope this book brings for friendship. And I'll trust that he does indeed know how it all turned out, and he's glad.

Elizabeth Foss

ACTIO

 **reach out**

Sit quietly for a few moments with this Scripture and essay and ask God to put on your heart the name of someone whom he wants you to befriend. What is he saying?

 **resolve**

How will you live out what God has shared with you in today's reading and essay?

 **rejoice**

At the end of this day, recount three blessings for which you are grateful.

1

2

3

prayer intentions

NAMES	INTENTIONS

DAILY SCRIPTURE
day three

Faithful friends are a sturdy shelter:
  whoever finds one has found a treasure.
Faithful friends are beyond price;
  no amount can balance their worth.
Faithful friends are life-saving medicine;
  and those who fear the Lord will find them.
Those who fear the Lord direct their friendship aright, for as they are, so are their neighbors also.

Sirach 6:14-17

for further study

Proverbs 20:5

lectio divina

LECTIO

SIRACH 6:14-17

Sirach is one of the deuterocanonical books of the Bible, meaning it's included in Catholic and Orthodox bibles, but not Protestant ones. Written by an unknown author between 200 and 175 BC, it is a collection of sayings that is deeply concerned with moral problems and offers guidance for all aspects of human life. In this chapter, the author offers advice on friendship—how to choose good friends, but also how to be a good friend to others.

MEDITATIO

What personal message does the text have for me?

ORATIO

What do I say to the Lord in response to his word?

CONTEMPLATIO

What conversion of mind, heart, and life is he asking of me today?

How did I progress in living the word today?

Several years ago a new neighbor and I decided to start running together. On the morning of our inaugural run, I was nervous because she looked like an Iron Woman athlete. When I'm nervous, I have the tendency to talk—a lot. So, as we ran at a quick clip, I yammered on and on. Afterwards, I felt winded not only from the physical exertion but also from my explosion of words.

Later that day I started stewing about my verbosity and decided to send an apology text. Well, it turns out she was grateful for my endless chatter because she said she was running so fast to keep up with me she could scarcely breathe. We both laughed at ourselves and admitted we were both so anxious about what the other might think that we ran much faster than our typical pace.

This woman not only became a loyal running companion. I count her among my dearest friends.

Amy and Katie are the kind of friends who have shown up at my doorstep with a meal in the wake of a family tragedy. I can talk to them about everything, from my toddler's diaper issues to thoughts about God. Even when we can't see each other as much as we'd like, we—as my teenager puts it—"very enthusiastically wave" at one another while passing by in our cars.

They're also the kind of friends I don't have to be a chameleon for; I never have to hide my true colors just to blend in. Instead, they know I'm socially awkward, that I sometimes lose my cool with my kids, and that I sweat like a man while running.

Every woman needs faithful friends who are "sturdy shelters" and "life-saving medicine." One of the strongest desires of the human heart is to belong—to have connection with our fellow human beings. You'd think, in this age of hyper-connectedness when we can easily find hundreds of like-minded "friends," that we'd feel more connected than ever. Yet I've found the opposite to be true. The more time we spend scrolling through carefully-curated social media feeds,

and the more effort we invest in creating our own online persona that reflects only the good and shiny parts of us, the more isolated we feel.

Truth is, we're hungrier than ever before for imperfect authenticity. So how do we find genuine friends—the kinds we'd never have to clean our house for? We start by living authentically ourselves, by not being so afraid of others' perceptions of us. Authentic friendship cannot be rooted in the fear of what others might think of you, your career, the state of your home, or what you feed your family. It must be rooted in love, trust, and acceptance.

Authenticity means admitting you're not an Olympic medalist and can't run like one. It means scratching beneath the Instagram surface and recognizing the humanity there. It means accepting we're all a part of the broken but beautiful body of Christ, and giving others permission to be less than perfect.

Instead of being rejected—what I fear might happen if I put my imperfect self out there—I've found I'm embraced when I send apology texts for incessant rambling, or I admit my kids sometimes drive me crazy. When we let our guard down, others can see us for who we really are. We're not superwomen. We are humans who depend upon God's supernatural grace.

Put yourself out there, my dear sister in Christ. That's exactly what I did when new neighbors moved in down the street. I was as awkward as ever. But they loved me anyway. And when you do find a steadfast sorority of women, give thanks and make sure you never get too busy to nurture those true friendships. A faithful friend is indeed priceless.

Kate Wicker

ACTIO

 **reach out**

Is there someone new to your neighborhood—a new mom you've never seen before in the pickup line at school, or waiting by the soccer field at the end of practice? Take a deep breath and welcome her genuinely. And if there really isn't, find someone online and jump outside the comment box and make a genuine personal connection.

 **resolve**

How will you live out what God has shared with you in today's reading and essay?

 **rejoice**

At the end of this day, recount three blessings for which you are grateful.

1

2

3

prayer intentions

NAMES	INTENTIONS

DAILY SCRIPTURE
day four

Therefore, my friends, since we have confidence to enter the sanctuary by the blood of Jesus, by the new and living way that he opened for us through the curtain (that is, through his flesh), and since we have a great priest over the house of God, let us approach with a true heart in full assurance of faith, with our hearts sprinkled clean from an evil conscience and our bodies washed with pure water. Let us hold fast to the confession of our hope without wavering, for he who has promised is faithful. And let us consider how to provoke one another to love and good deeds, not neglecting to meet together, as is the habit of some, but encouraging one another, and all the more as you see the Day approaching.

Hebrews 10:19-25

for further study

Acts 2:42-47

lectio divina

LECTIO

HEBREWS 10:19-25

Composed by an unknown author before the fall of Jerusalem in 70 AD, Hebrews ties Old Testament history and practice to the life and ministry of Jesus. Ancient belief holds that the letter was written to Jewish converts to Christianity, and the book itself is a complex study of Christology, focusing on the priesthood and sacrifice of Christ. In these verses, the author discusses the importance of friendship for fellowship and mutual encouragement in living the Christian life.

MEDITATIO

What personal message does the text have for me?

ORATIO

What do I say to the Lord in response to his word?

CONTEMPLATIO

What conversion of mind, heart, and life is he asking of me today?

How did I progress in living the word today?

It felt like it came out of nowhere. I was shocked and confused at what seemed like the abrupt end of a close friendship. But I see now that the loss really happened slowly, over time. Like a tire that's worn down until it eventually blows out, I had noticed that things felt slightly off here and there, but I didn't realize the full extent of the damage until too late.

Any relationship that we don't nurture enough will eventually fade away, and I had stopped nurturing this one. At the time, my life was especially overwhelming. My husband had a demanding job, I was struggling with a difficult pregnancy, and, in my third trimester, our house flooded, and we had to move out for several weeks.

The more chaotic things got, the more I neglected to return my friend's phone calls and texts. It wasn't that I didn't miss her; there just always seemed to be a reason it wasn't a good time to connect. I assumed that we'd be able to pick right back up once I had more time, but I'd failed to consider how much my absence would hurt her, or how much she needed our friendship during those months. And it wasn't until after the chaos settled a bit that I realized how much I'd needed her encouraging words and support during that time as well.

Some friendships can be restored and re-started when the timing improves, but many cannot. When we make someone feel that we have no space for them in our lives, we can irrevocably alter that relationship. That doesn't mean that we can't come to those we've hurt in humility and ask for their forgiveness. But whenever we stop reaching out or responding to a friend, the hard truth is that we risk losing them altogether.

These days, life is still chaotic. That's just how it is much of the time for most of us. I've accepted that I can't possibly stay close to every once-close friend. It's just not feasible. But I've also learned from that first painful loss. When a relationship is authentic and full of mutual encouragement, like that friendship was, I take the time to maintain it, even when it's hard and requires extra effort.

Taking the time to call a friend after the kids go to bed means occasionally letting the laundry and dishes wait. Getting to my weekly Bible study with friends means waking my children earlier than usual and planning ahead. And asking my husband to take on extra caregiving duties so I can travel across states to be with a suffering friend takes humility and lots of preparation. But working through those obstacles shows faithfulness to my friends and also strengthens my faith through the life-giving gift of human connection. And when a friendship has been nurtured, it allows us to trust that our friend will be there in our times of need.

Living a Christian life is not easy. But God gave us sisters and brothers in Christ so that we might support one another along the way. It is through this mutual encouragement that we "provoke one another to love and good deeds" (Hebrews 10:24).

Yet, for any of this to happen, we must first show up for one another. So let us give the gift of our presence, mirroring the faithfulness that God shows us in the way we offer ourselves, again and again. Even if our responsibilities leave us little time and energy to offer, let us not neglect those relationships completely. We need our friends and they need us. And we can trust with confidence that even our small offerings of love will be amplified by God, encouraging and strengthening each other in big and powerful ways.

Allison McGinley

ACTIO

 **reach out**

Who is that friend you've been meaning to call, the one you're sure will still be there when things settle down? Talk, text, or visit her today!

 **resolve**

How will you live out what God has shared with you in today's reading and essay?

 **rejoice**

At the end of this day, recount three blessings for which you are grateful.

1

2

3

prayer intentions

NAMES	INTENTIONS

DAILY SCRIPTURE
day five

Paul and Timothy, servants of Christ Jesus, To all the saints in Christ Jesus who are in Philippi, with the bishops and deacons: Grace to you and peace from God our Father and the Lord Jesus Christ.

I thank my God every time I remember you, constantly praying with joy in every one of my prayers for all of you, because of your sharing in the gospel from the first day until now. I am confident of this, that the one who began a good work among you will bring it to completion by the day of Jesus Christ. It is right for me to think this way about all of you, because you hold me in your heart, for all of you share in God's grace with me, both in my imprisonment and in the defense and confirmation of the gospel. For God is my witness, how I long for all of you with the compassion of Christ Jesus. And this is my prayer, that your love may overflow more and more with knowledge and full insight to help you to determine what is best, so that in the day of Christ you may be pure and blameless, having produced the harvest of righteousness that comes through Jesus Christ for the glory and praise of God.

Philippians 1:1-11

for further study
2 Thessalonians 1:3

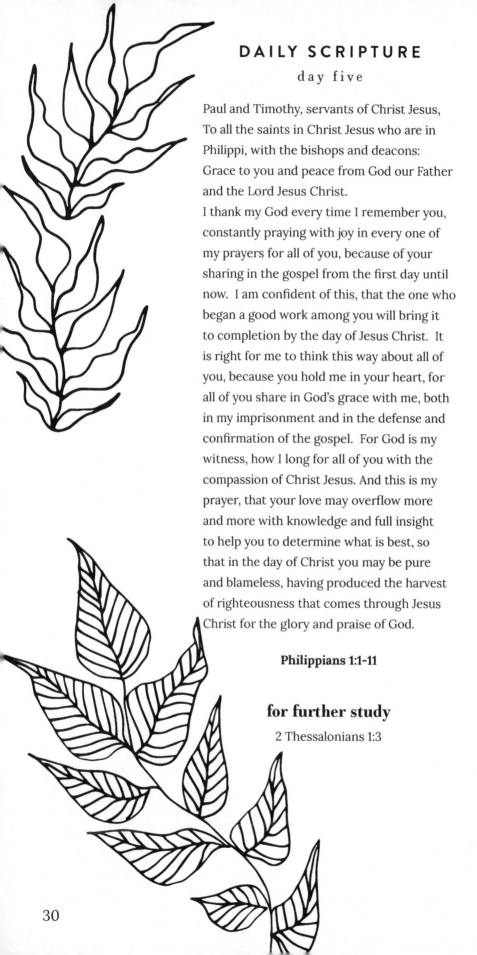

lectio divina

LECTIO

PHILIPPIANS 1:1-11

The "epistle of joy", St. Paul wrote this letter to the people of Philippi, a major city in Macedonia (in modern-day Greece), in 62 AD. Even though he is writing from prison, Paul does not let this affect his spirits; the letter to the Philippians overflows with joy and thanksgiving for the thriving Christian community in Philippi. Here, St. Paul thanks the Philippians for their friendship and partnership in the work of spreading the gospel and for their support during his imprisonment.

MEDITATIO

What personal message does the text have for me?

ORATIO

What do I say to the Lord in response to his word?

CONTEMPLATIO

What conversion of mind, heart, and life is he asking of me today?

How did I progress in living the word today?

To belong—to be known and loved to our depths even at our darkest—is one of the greatest desires of the human heart. In my own life this desire has led to much heartache, but also to ultimate triumph. My longing to belong somewhere, to someone, led me to Jesus.

Growing up Indian and Hindu in small town Iowa, I was the one classmate ridiculed because not only was I a nerd, but I was different. The sting of hurt lingers when I remember being asked to dance as a prank. I was the one whose invitations were rarely answered, and whose invitations to parties never came. I struggled through with a small group of friends, but at my core, I was deeply lonely.

These experiences shaped how I formed friendships into adulthood. The longing to belong grew, but the depth to which I revealed my heart lessened day by day. I pursued belonging in fleeting (and harmful) ways. Ultimately, after stumbling on the shallow way to "friendship," I was empty. I didn't need another party that made me feel like I belonged for a moment, only to wake up lonelier the next day. I needed a friend—one who knew my longing and understood what was behind it. It was during this time that my friend Gina invited me to church. The rest, as they say, is history.

Gina was the first to see behind the façade. She also knew what it was to long for more and brought me to the only place that would fill the empty space in me. Our friendship has ebbed and flowed through the years as we've navigated work, relocations, marriage, children, and heartaches. There have been years when the demands of life created distance. As we have grown older, I have come to know the deep joy of a friendship nurtured by grace.

C.S. Lewis writes in *The Four Loves*, "Friendship is born at the moment when one says to another 'What! You too? I thought that no one but myself . . .'" My childhood experiences of feeling isolated in my "weirdness" kept me locked inside myself. I was imprisoned by the fear of ending up alone if I shared my deepest desires and fears. I had no idea of the beauty that is born when spirit shares with spirit. I had

bought into the lie that having a wide social circle filled my need to belong. Thankfully, God, in his wisdom and mercy, showed me how wrong I was.

He sent me women who repeatedly show me I am not alone. Through the student who frequented my office and grew into the sister I never had, and women who invited me to sit outside a ballroom in Charleston and became my tribe, God has shown me it is precisely in sharing our deepest fears and desires that we create the strongest bonds. We cannot hold one another in our hearts, as St. Paul writes, if we never share them. These friendships, born of "shared weirdness," are the ones that remind me God is doing a good work in me when I forget. They also give me a kick in the seat and nudge me back on track when I have strayed.

I've heard Fr. John Riccardo say friendship is time wasted together looking in the same direction. These are not five-minute friendships born at random events. As Christian women, they are born of intentional time shared walking together toward Christ. So often our wounds keep us locked away from one another in fear, when instead they could become a window to grace-filled friendship. That fear doesn't subside overnight, but rather, one baby step of faith at a time. Take that first step today. Extend an invitation of grace amid the fear of vulnerability. Somewhere, someone is waiting to say, "What? You too? I thought I was the only one…"

Rahki McCormick

ACTIO

 **reach out**

In the still and the quiet of some moment today, re-read today's Scripture. Are you imprisoned by your fears, and still hurt by old wounds? Who is the person you can invite to visit you there? How can allow yourself to be vulnerable and to let someone else bind those wounds?

 **resolve**

How will you live out what God has shared with you in today's reading and essay?

 **rejoice**

At the end of this day, recount three blessings for which you are grateful.

1

2

3

prayer intentions

NAMES	INTENTIONS

DAILY SCRIPTURE
day six

Finally, all of you, have unity of spirit, sympathy, love for one another, a tender heart, and a humble mind. Do not repay evil for evil or abuse for abuse; but, on the contrary, repay with a blessing. It is for this that you were called—that you might inherit a blessing.

1 Peter 3:8-9

for further study

Matthew 23:10-12

lectio divina

LECTIO

1 PETER 3:8-9

One of the New Testament's catholic epistles, meaning it was addressed to all Christians rather than a specific church, First Peter was written in the early 60s AD. The author, who is traditionally identified as St. Peter, exhorts the faithful to remain strong amidst rising hostility and adversity. Today's verses remind the faithful to dwell in unity and love one another, since love is the foundation of a truly Christian life.

MEDITATIO

What personal message does the text have for me?

ORATIO

What do I say to the Lord in response to his word?

CONTEMPLATIO

What conversion of mind, heart, and life is he asking of me today?

How did I progress in living the word today?

My two older sisters are two years apart in age. I came along more than nine years later. While I've always loved all my older siblings, I have also often felt I didn't quite blend into the group like the four of them who were so close in age did, especially my sisters. When I added long years spent overseas missing many family events that create a shared history, that perceived difference grew even more glaring in my eyes.

In the last ten months since I returned to the United States from the mission field, my perception has shifted. I have more contact with my sisters; as my boys have grown and I have returned to working outside my home full time, our lives more closely resemble each other's. In the past few months, as we have mourned the death of our mother, and I have walked through a heavy personal crisis, a remarkable blessing has been discovering the deep, abiding and true friendship that I have with my sisters.

Today, two surprise packages filled with cheer arrived on my front porch, one from each of my sisters. Just before these arrived I had reached out by text to let them both know how much I appreciate their support and love. It was a joyful collision of the grace of true friendship.

When Scripture speaks to us of life in relationship with others, the words "unity" and references to "being one," either in mind or spirit, are repeated often. In today's verses, Peter refers to "unity of spirit." What brings about the experience of unity of spirit, that moment when we interact with one another with a pure and singular intention?

Here, Peter tells us that it is having sympathy and love for one another, tender hearts and humble minds. When we can enter into the moment and put ourselves in the place where someone else's spirit resides, have sympathy for her, and then love her right there where we find her, we are united because we choose to make her experience our common, shared experience. When we approach the world with tender-heartedness and humility, we live open to relationship. We look at the people around us through the lens of Christ-like

love, allowing ourselves to be drawn into their hearts by the openness of our own. We build friendships based in a unity of spirit that comes from a wellspring of tenderness, cultivated in our hearts by the grace of our Savior's love for us.

Friendships founded on that kind of loving union of spirits become a place not only of shared experience, but of deeply shared sorrow and shared hope, of shared vision and shared faith. They become tender spaces in our lives where we know we are held in the heart of another.

My sisters have been the greatest reminders to me in recent months of that kind of love. As they have offered sympathy and tenderhearted grace to me, I have humbly realized that my assumption—that I could never be drawn into the depth of friendship they shared—was wholeheartedly incorrect. The entering in has nothing to do with our differences, only with our willingness to open our hearts to the love being offered and to reciprocate in kind. When we do, we find ourselves giving and receiving from one another with fluidity and ease, the kind that shows up on our front porch to bolster a drooping spirit and simultaneously lights up a phone with gratitude in the same summer afternoon—grace bumping into itself on its way in and out of our overflowing hearts. Unity of spirit, indeed.

Colleen Mitchell

ACTIO

 **reach out**

Arrange for a front-porch affirmation of friendship. It doesn't have to be expensive or fancy. Send a favorite paperback to arrive at the home of a faraway friend or just show up with a store-bought bouquet or a latte you made at home on the porch of a local friend. Serendipitous occasions of grace begin with one party taking one step forward into God's design.

 **resolve**

How will you live out what God has shared with you in today's reading and essay?

 **rejoice**

At the end of this day, recount three blessings for which you are grateful.

1

2

3

prayer intentions

NAMES	INTENTIONS

day seven

Selah is a Hebrew word found often in the psalms and a few times in Habakkuk. Scholars aren't absolutely certain what it means. It seems to be a musical or liturgical note—maybe a pause or maybe a crescendo.

We have set aside this space—this day—for you to use as your selah. Perhaps you pause here and just review what you have pondered thus far. Perhaps you rejoice here and use the space for shouts of praise. Or maybe you take the opportunity to fill in some gaps in the pages before this one.

It's your space. Selah. Give it meaning.

scripture
MEMORY
week two
day eight

Scripture is God's conversation with us, and it's the truest thing we'll hear in this life. When we memorize it, we carry his voice into every moment of our existence.

This week we are reminded that Christ's sacrifice was the gift of his entire self. We can ask ourselves how we can give so selflessly in our own lives.

· · · ·

"This is my commandment, that you love one another as I have loved you. No one has greater love than this, to lay down one's life for one's friends. You are my friends if you do what I command you.

JOHN 15:12-14

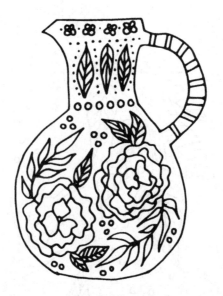

DAILY SCRIPTURE
day nine

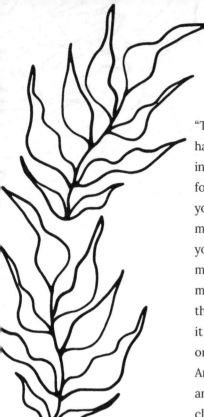

"Then the king will say to those at his right hand, 'Come, you that are blessed by my Father, inherit the kingdom prepared for you from the foundation of the world; for I was hungry and you gave me food, I was thirsty and you gave me something to drink, I was a stranger and you welcomed me, I was naked and you gave me clothing, I was sick and you took care of me, I was in prison and you visited me.' Then the righteous will answer him, 'Lord, when was it that we saw you hungry and gave you food, or thirsty and gave you something to drink? And when was it that we saw you a stranger and welcomed you, or naked and gave you clothing? And when was it that we saw you sick or in prison and visited you?' And the king will answer them, 'Truly I tell you, just as you did it to one of the least of these who are members of my family, you did it to me.'"

Matthew 25:34-40

for further study

Luke 6:37-38

lectio divina

LECTIO

MATTHEW 25:34-40

In his Gospel, Matthew stresses the new covenant and law that Jesus brings, one that deeply stresses interior holiness and brotherly love. In today's verses, Jesus speaks about this love, noting that those who care for the poor and afflicted also care for him.

MEDITATIO

What personal message does the text have for me?

ORATIO

What do I say to the Lord in response to his word?

CONTEMPLATIO

What conversion of mind, heart, and life is he asking of me today?

How did I progress in living the word today?

I vividly remember the first time she said those words. I was in the garage, pulling a frozen casserole from the freezer. A veteran of hyperemesis gravidarum, one of my coping strategies was to begin cooking in large batches the moment the pregnancy test turned pink. That way, I'd have the freezer stocked before the nausea hit, and I could feed my family without actually cooking during those awful months of debilitating sickness.

I wasn't nauseated as I pulled this comfort food from the depths of the deep freeze, though. The nausea had subsided shortly after the sonogram confirmed no beating heart. Instead, I was numbly moving through the day, thawing a part of my recently frozen stash while I organized my household before surgery. I hadn't told anyone outside my four walls about this baby, and my plan was to power through without bothering a soul with the news of our loss. Further, this coming week was supposed to be one of celebration, and I was a mom with a sacrament to celebrate and a party to throw.

It was the week before my daughter's First Communion, and there were several special weeknight moments planned at our Catechesis of the Good Shepherd atrium. Anticipating being unable to get her there the next day, I'd called her teacher to ask for a ride. I didn't share the particulars of my need. I just made sure my daughter wouldn't miss a moment of her special week. She assured me that she'd take care of Mary Beth, and then, as I was just about to say goodbye, she said those words.

"What can I do for you?"

I was surprised. After all, we'd just confirmed that she was providing transportation for my daughter.

"I'm sorry," I stammered. "What do you mean?"

"What can I do for you?" she repeated.

And I sat on the garage steps, and wept.

What I would learn, over more than fifteen years of friendship, is that the phrase she repeated for me that day is my friend Jen's trademark phrase. Those five words are the ones spoken from her heart into the lives of people she loves. Those are the words she used to open to me the gift of herself offered in friendship.

Over the years, we have served one another in some of the darkest moments a woman can imagine. Sometimes, service was the gracious hospitality of a house at the beach when I needed a quiet retreat. Once, it was a favorite takeout hamburger, ironically purchased by me despite my extreme hyperemesis two years after the first conversation, and taken to her when life hurt so much that she could not eat. Jen spoke those words all those years ago, but more than that, she taught me to speak them, too.

Our Lord suggests so many ways that we can serve one another. At first, the list seems like a "choose the one the best suits you" kind of menu. Friends like Jen have taught me otherwise. That list is a warning. To be a friend in the name of Christ is to be open to the possibility that you will be called upon to serve in any (or all) of the ways that he mentions.

Further, Jesus challenges us to say Jen's brave words aloud and to invite the inconvenience, the pain, the sacrifice, and the emotional investment that comes with genuinely reaching out and being open to having someone else tell you how to serve.

You want to be a friend, but you don't know how to serve?

Ask.

Utter those brave and very specific words, and repeat them, if necessary, to let someone else know that you mean it: you're there to genuinely offer the gift of your service.

Elizabeth Foss

ACTIO

 **reach out**

Today, say Jen's words aloud to someone. See how they open your heart. *What can I do for you?*

 **resolve**

How will you live out what God has shared with you in today's reading and essay?

 **rejoice**

At the end of this day, recount three blessings for which you are grateful.

1

2

3

prayer intentions

NAMES	INTENTIONS

DAILY SCRIPTURE
day ten

We know love by this, that he laid down his life for us—and we ought to lay down our lives for one another. How does God's love abide in anyone who has the world's goods and sees a brother or sister in need and yet refuses help?
Little children, let us love, not in word or speech, but in truth and action.

1 John 3:16-18

for further study

1 Corinthians 12:24-26

lectio divina

LECTIO

1 JOHN 3:16-18

Another of the catholic epistles, St. John wrote this letter from Ephesus (now part of Turkey) probably around 90-100 AD, after he had composed his Gospel. The letter is written to unnamed churches in Ephesus in order to correct false teachers who were leading the believers into error. John stresses that the great commandment of Christians is to love one another; in today's verses, John calls us not to the martyrdom of death, but living martyrdom, which involves a lifetime of sacrifice for the love of others, as Jesus' life was for us.

MEDITATIO

What personal message does the text have for me?

ORATIO

What do I say to the Lord in response to his word?

CONTEMPLATIO

What conversion of mind, heart, and life is he asking of me today?

How did I progress in living the word today?

When the Bible talks about service, it's easy to mentally jump to the big, splashy things: going to Uganda to serve among orphans and the destitute, working in Siberia at a TB clinic, volunteering at the local homeless shelter, or organizing a food drive. And those are all needed and important activities.

But do we think about service to our friends? I'd guess not, in the normal course of life.

In Charles Dickens' novel *Bleak House*, there is a character called Mrs. Jellyby. She has a large family, full of people and things that need her attention, but her focus is always on her "Borrioboola-Gha venture." She spends her days sending out literature and writing letters about the needs of an obscure African tribe. While that's commendable, she ignores the needs of her husband and her children in order to "serve" strangers. She's missing her real vocation—the service right in front of her face. By the end of the novel, Mr. Jellyby is almost suicidal, and one of the Jellyby daughters says that she's come to hate the very word "Africa," because it's synonymous with her mother's fanatical project.

I think we can be Mrs. Jellyby when it comes to our friends' needs. Our friends, usually, have food and clothes and water. When a crisis pops up, we can certainly bring dinner and offer rides and child care and household help. Sometimes, though, our friends need heart help. Sometimes our friends need a Christmas tree.

One of my best friends in high school was Sue. Her mom had breast cancer, which she'd been fighting for more than ten years. Sue's father was always busy with work or taking her mother to appointments. So Sue took on most of the household chores, on top of all her school work and extracurriculars.

One night, while we were hanging out in her kitchen baking cookies, she said that her family wasn't planning on putting up their tree this year. They might not even celebrate Christmas. It was just too much work. She told me this very clinically, without any emotion, but I knew that it bothered her.

"We are going to put the tree up ourselves," I announced. And we did. We spent the rest of that Friday night putting up the artificial tree, hanging lights and old family ornaments that had appeared on her family's tree since Sue was a baby. The tree was smallish, maybe five feet tall, and stood in the corner of the family room along the wood-panelled wall. When it was up, the family room no longer felt sad and neglected and worn down. It felt hopeful.

At the time, I didn't think putting up the tree was service. But spending time with Sue, just being with her and doing normal teenage things—I see now that that was service. That was love. Bringing a bit of extra joy into my friend's life cost me nothing except attention.

When St. John talks about "love...in truth and action," I think he means Christmas trees. I think he means cups of coffee over kitchen tables, or bringing movies to a friend's house when she's had a bad week and having a movie marathon while eating super-salty popcorn (a regular treat for me and my best friend). It's going to see movies where there's limited plot and lots of things blow up because studying for the bar exam is intensely stressful and the cure for that is the new *Mission: Impossible* movie. It's text messages that just say "hi" and send love on the spur of the moment.

Our service doesn't have to be big and splashy to be real love. It can cost nothing but time and eye contact. Often, that's worth more than anything else.

Emily DeArdo

ACTIO

 **reach out**

Do a mental scan of your friends (and maybe even your neighbors who are not yet friends). Who could use a simple pick-me-up? How you can you bless someone locally without a lot of fuss and fanfare?

 **resolve**

How will you live out what God has shared with you in today's reading and essay?

 **rejoice**

At the end of this day, recount three blessings for which you are grateful.

1

2

3

prayer intentions

NAMES	INTENTIONS

DAILY SCRIPTURE
day eleven

Likewise, tell the older women to be reverent in behavior, not to be slanderers or slaves to drink; they are to teach what is good, so that they may encourage the young women to love their husbands, to love their children, to be self-controlled, chaste, good managers of the household, kind, being submissive to their husbands, so that the word of God may not be discredited.

Titus 2:3-5

for further study

Hebrews 13:7

lectio divina

LECTIO

TITUS 2:3-5

Titus is one of the pastoral epistles, so called because in these letters, St. Paul is concerned with the pastoral care of the early Christian community. Titus may have been composed between 63-66 AD, and the letter encourages Titus to stand firm in the teachings and doctrine of the faith as he builds up the local church. St. Paul notes that faith and life should be one whole—the behavior Paul expects is part of the "sound doctrine" he mentions in verse 2:1. Our lives must be consistent with our beliefs.

MEDITATIO

What personal message does the text have for me?

ORATIO

What do I say to the Lord in response to his word?

CONTEMPLATIO

What conversion of mind, heart, and life is he asking of me today?

How did I progress in living the word today?

I distinctly remember the first time someone called me a Titus 2 woman. I was thirty-four, and I immediately disqualified myself. I could not possibly be the "older woman" of this passage! Primarily because, thirty-four was hardly old, and secondly, the Titus 2 woman has it all figured out, no matter what "it" is. I could not possibly be a mentor because I was still wrestling with big questions and little ones, and I was still learning so many things every day.

Over time, I began to accept the role in some situations. I could see how I did have wisdom born of experience to pass along. By the time I was forty, I'd birthed eight babies, and I'd experienced unmedicated, emergency c-section, and VBAC births, so I could see how maybe I was "qualified" to share birth experiences. I'd breastfed and raised those babies through toddlerhood and early childhood and the first few were finishing high school. So, maybe I had a thing or two to impart. But it would still be a decade more before I began to feel comfortably old enough to mentor.

And then I met Valerie.

Valerie is fourteen years younger than I am. We were seated together at a bridal luncheon—Valerie with her elderly mother-in-law and me with my mother. Over the course of two hours, I watched as Valerie talked with each lady. At first, I was just absorbing small talk, but then I noticed how incredibly gifted and skilled Valerie was at dignifying and honoring both women, bringing both hopefulness and good cheer into a conversation that had distinct holes where cognition and capability should be. I listened to her talk about family life and her children, and I was enraptured by her grace and her obvious joy. I wanted to ask her where I could sign up to learn to be the lovely, gracious woman she clearly was.

A Titus 2 woman doesn't have to have a lengthy resume and gray hair. A Titus 2 woman only has to be a mentor of love. When we look for women to be our Titus 2 friends, we look at the fruits of the Spirit in their lives. The word tells us to see what the outcome of their way of life is and then (assuming

that that outcome is rich with the Lord's fullness), to imitate their way of faith. (Hebrews 13:7)

For such a short passage, we find very clear guidance for choosing mentors in these words in Titus. God is not leaving anything to chance here; he wants us to clearly understand how important it is to be discriminating when we choose the women we want to shepherd us in the Christian way of womanhood, and he wants us to be equally careful when we influence other women.

The call to be a mentor is one of enormous importance. Reaching out to other women and sharing our own failures and the lessons they yielded, our own successes and the fruits they bore: that's where the real exchange of faith happens. That's where women build the Church. We are all called to mentor.

Before we go out preaching and teaching from the street corners, however, we have to remember that we are all called to holiness first. God asks us to share with one another and to make disciples of each other, but he reminds us in no uncertain terms that he expects us to hold ourselves to a standard of holy behavior. When you choose a mentor, choose a holy one. When you are a mentor, be a holy one.

None of us will do this perfectly. None of us will ever feel entirely qualified to mentor someone else. (If we do, we can be assured that we have not fully assessed our own weaknesses.) But all of us can know that with God's grace, no matter our age or station in life, we have something both to receive and to offer other women in the lifelong journey to become women of God.

Elizabeth Foss

ACTIO

 **reach out**

Who is a woman in your life who has taught you more deeply what it means to love? Find a way to thank her today—with a hand-written note, a call or text, an invitation to get together, or a simple prayer offered on her behalf. Let her know how much you appreciate her role as a "Titus 2 woman" in your life.

 **resolve**

How will you live out what God has shared with you in today's reading and essay?

 **rejoice**

At the end of this day, recount three blessings for which you are grateful.

1

2

3

prayer intentions

NAMES	INTENTIONS

DAILY SCRIPTURE
day twelve

Now as they went on their way, he entered a certain village, where a woman named Martha welcomed him into her home. She had a sister named Mary, who sat at the Lord's feet and listened to what he was saying. But Martha was distracted by her many tasks; so she came to him and asked, "Lord, do you not care that my sister has left me to do all the work by myself? Tell her then to help me." But the Lord answered her, "Martha, Martha, you are worried and distracted by many things; there is need of only one thing. Mary has chosen the better part, which will not be taken away from her."

Luke 10:38-42

for further study

Matthew 6:33

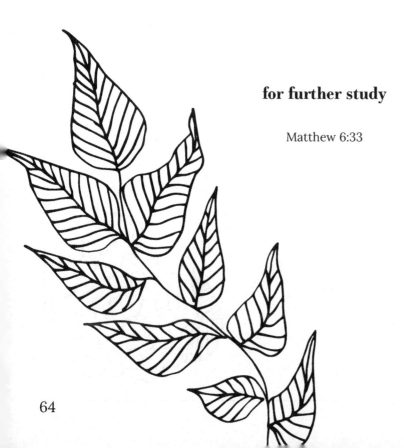

lectio divina

LUKE 10:38-42

Written sometime in the 80s AD, St. Luke's Gospel was written for Gentile Christians and is considered the most literary gospel. It is also unique in that it gives women prominent places in the narrative, such as today's verses focused on Mary and Martha. There is also an emphasis on the interior life of prayer, which is seen here, when Jesus stresses that Mary has correctly made Jesus the center of her attention. No matter how busy our lives are, Jesus and the life of prayer must come first.

LECTIO

MEDITATIO

What personal message does the text have for me?

ORATIO

What do I say to the Lord in response to his word?

CONTEMPLATIO

What conversion of mind, heart, and life is he asking of me today?

How did I progress in living the word today?

I have long resisted the plethora of Christian titles that provide instruction and insight on "how to be a Mary" for those of us whose natural inclination is to be a Martha, or, more accurately, for every woman whose daily duties require she spend a majority of her time in service to others, no matter what her natural inclination is. Because if we look at the story told here, what we see is that Martha was not simply running around distracted by her own whims. People had gathered in her home around an important teacher whom many of them were beginning to identify as the Messiah. Family and friends sat in her home listening intently. And they needed to drink and eat. Martha's duty was to serve out of both her love for them and her friendship with Jesus.

This is a perfect picture of my own life most days. Christ is present and waiting for me, sure, but in addition, a throng of people are also present and waiting for me—to drive them to school, to teach them, to feed them, to encourage them or collaborate with them, to turn in a manuscript, to respond to their emails. I work in my home to serve my family, and I work outside my home in service to others that also provides a service to my family. I *provide* for people. And the work that this duty requires of me is far from a whimsical distraction. It is my vocation. It is my path to sanctity.

So while I may or may not be a Martha by nature, I am a Martha by vocation and there is no way around that. However, what I have come to realize is that the Martha-Mary comparison is not an either-or proposition, but a both-and invitation. When Jesus tells a flustered and irritated Martha that she is "worried and distracted by many things" while Mary "has chosen the better part, which will not be taken from her," I do not think he is rebuking us for honoring our duty to serve the friends who make their way through our doors looking for Christ; after all, he is the Savior we recognize in the breaking of the bread. He's all for sharing a meal with his friends.

I think rather than looking at Martha as a woman in need of correction, Jesus is looking at all of us as women in need of invitation—an invitation to set aside irritation and worry

and frustration and notice him present amid our activities, speaking to us as we serve. Martha had the opportunity to cook and serve those in her home and still choose the better part of placing her heart and mind at the feet of Jesus. It was not Martha's service that distracted her from his presence, but her anxiety and worry over her long to-do list. Jesus was not asking her to become Mary, but to become the best version of Martha. And he is inviting you to become the best version of yourself as you serve him through your daily duties, to infuse those acts of service with a prayerful, docile spirit rather than anxiety and worry. To work with intention and offer your service in love rather than irritation. And to be content in who you are because you know who he is. Can you hear the invitation being offered to you today? Come, slow down, and be made joyful by the Messiah's good news, alive and active in your home, in your heart, and in the service you are called to provide.

Colleen Mitchell

ACTIO

 **reach out**

Grant yourself some grace today. Give yourself permission to take Jesus up on his invitation to set aside your preoccupations and notice him. He is the one reaching out. Just sit at his feet and absorb his presence.

 **resolve**

How will you live out what God has shared with you in today's reading and essay?

 **rejoice**

At the end of this day, recount three blessings for which you are grateful.

1

2

3

prayer intentions

NAMES	INTENTIONS

DAILY SCRIPTURE
day thirteen

So Jesus called them and said to them, "You know that among the Gentiles those whom they recognize as their rulers lord it over them, and their great ones are tyrants over them. But it is not so among you; but whoever wishes to become great among you must be your servant, and whoever wishes to be first among you must be slave of all. For the Son of Man came not to be served but to serve, and to give his life a ransom for many."

Mark 10:42-45

for further study

Galatians 5:13

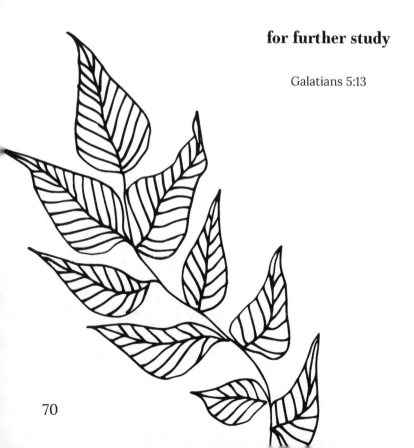

lectio divina

LECTIO

MARK 10:42-45

The Gospel of Mark was written by John Mark, a disciple of Peter, around 60 AD, and was aimed at the community of Gentile Christians in Rome. It is the shortest gospel, written in a streamlined fashion, with St. Peter as its main source. Mark stresses both the good news of Christ, but also the cost of discipleship, as we see in today's verses. Real Christian service involves humility and following Christ, even at the cost of our lives.

MEDITATIO

What personal message does the text have for me?

ORATIO

What do I say to the Lord in response to his word?

CONTEMPLATIO

What conversion of mind, heart, and life is he asking of me today?

How did I progress in living the word today?

Sometimes our Lord shows up in dark places, and calls out to us to meet him there, to serve him and to be served by him through our friendships.

My closest friend recently suffered her first miscarriage. Contrary to the planned service I often give to friends through signing up on a "Take Them a Meal" list, I was called to drop everything to serve this friend in her darkest of times. I was completely heartbroken for her; the love I felt for her, and for her little one that she would never meet, was deep, and that made it easy to reach out and serve her—to bind her wounds as Christ did, but also to see her as Christ in my life. There was an automatic deepening of friendship that occured in and through this service, for which I am so thankful.

I could see the hand of God even more clearly through this situation when, just a few short weeks later, I suffered my third consecutive miscarriage; this friend was there immediately. She served me through her words, through her service in bringing me a meal, and by taking care of my children. She was Christ to me, and I received her gifts.

It is in and through these spontaneous acts of love that God sows some of the most beautiful, fruitful seeds of deeper friendship, of bonds that cannot easily be broken. It is here that we truly meet Christ in his passion, when we are called both to be Christ to our friends and to serve them as though they were Christ himself.

Our Lord says in Mark, "For the Son of man also came not to be served but to serve, and to give his life as a ransom for many." (Mark 10:45) The Son of Man. God himself, he came to serve us, to lay down his life for us. This ought to be the most defining characteristic of our friendships: life-giving service, and acceptance of this service from our friends.

The temptation of pride in resisting the service of others and not allowing them to be Christ to us is a real one. For years, I was reluctant to allow others to help me in any way other than accepting meals after we had children. Offers from friends to take my kids for a few hours, or to get me

groceries when friends knew I was struggling were turned down because of my pride; I wanted to give the impression that I had it more together than I really did. Further, I didn't want to relinquish whatever control I felt like I had. Charity in friendship is not limited to being the one giving; it is humbling ourselves, admitting our weakness and needs, and allowing our friends to serve us.

Our Lord accepted the service of others on his way of the cross, and this was the beginning of friendship for him. The service that Simon of Cyrene was pressed into for our Lord was likely unexpected for him, a spontaneous act of self-gift, which may have even been given tentatively. St. Josemaría Escrivá writes in *The Way of the Cross* that:

> ...in the whole context of the passion this help does not add up to very much. But for Jesus, a smile, a word, a gesture, a little bit of love is enough for Him to pour out His grace bountifully on the soul of His friend.

It is in giving and receiving these smiles, words, gestures, and small services in our friendships that Jesus pours his grace bountifully into our souls, making our friendships deeper and holier.

Ana Hahn

ACTIO

 **reach out**

Think about the twofold nature of service in Christ. Which way will you be like Jesus today: will you serve or will you allow someone to serve you?

 **resolve**

How will you live out what God has shared with you in today's reading and essay?

 **rejoice**

At the end of this day, recount three blessings for which you are grateful.

1

2

3

prayer intentions

NAMES	INTENTIONS

day fourteen

Selah is a Hebrew word found often in the psalms and a few times in Habakkuk. Scholars aren't absolutely certain what it means. It seems to be a musical or liturgical note—maybe a pause or maybe a crescendo.

We have set aside this space—this day—for you to use as your selah. Perhaps you pause here and just review what you have pondered thus far. Perhaps you rejoice here and use the space for shouts of praise. Or maybe you take the opportunity to fill in some gaps in the pages before this one.

It's your space. Selah. Give it meaning.

scripture
MEMORY
week three
day fifteen

Are you memorizing? Are you surprised that the Holy Spirit is with you in this endeavor and you really can commit chunks of wisdom to your memory? It takes some work, but it yields such rich treasure!

This week's selection is a little longer, but it's a such good reminder as we navigate the world of relationships that it's worth the extra effort.

....

My friends, if anyone is detected in a transgression, you who have received the Spirit should restore such a one in a spirit of gentleness. Take care that you yourselves are not tempted.
Bear one another's burdens, and in this way you will fulfill the law of Christ.
For if those who are nothing think they are something, they deceive themselves.
All must test their own work; then that work, rather than
their neighbor's work, will become a cause for pride.
For all must carry their own loads.
Those who are taught the word must share in all good things with their teacher.

GALATIANS 6:1-6

GALATIANS 6:2

DAILY SCRIPTURE
day sixteen

If then there is any encouragement in Christ, any consolation from love, any sharing in the Spirit, any compassion and sympathy, make my joy complete: be of the same mind, having the same love, being in full accord and of one mind. Do nothing from selfish ambition or conceit, but in humility regard others as better than yourselves. Let each of you look not to your own interests, but to the interests of others. Let the same mind be in you that was in Christ Jesus...

Philippians 2:1-5

for further study

Proverbs 27:2

lectio divina

LECTIO

PHILIPPIANS 2:1-5

The letter to the Philippians teaches us about genuine Christian living. In today's verses, St. Paul encourages the Philippians to remain united and show their love for each other through humility and service, just as Christ did.

MEDITATIO

What personal message does the text have for me?

ORATIO

What do I say to the Lord in response to his word?

CONTEMPLATIO

What conversion of mind, heart, and life is he asking of me today?

How did I progress in living the word today?

There are women who struggle to open the doors of their homes to one another. We think that if we have to kick the stray shoes out of the way to open the front door or sweep the unfolded laundry from the couch into a basket before you can sit down, that you will find us lacking. We think that you will not love us because of our imperfections. And you know something else? There are women who struggle to open their hearts for just the same reason.

We focus so hard on what you will think of us if you know our faults, our failures, our dark places, and our deep fears, that we keep them safely locked up. If we don't open that door, and you can't come in, then everything stays safe and pretty on the outside.

In the meantime, you shiver in the cold on the front stoop.

Over time, I have learned to shout down the lies I believed about friendship, and so, to open the door more and more. I know now that friendship isn't a performance. It's not an opportunity to impress. Friendship isn't a call to be the most polished, presentable version of myself. It's not carefully kept, and tidy and pretty. Friendship isn't only for the people who meet the impossible standard to which I hold myself.

The freedom in friendship comes when I befriend the real, broken, imperfect, and needy people God puts in my path. The freedom in friendship comes when I recognize that I don't have to be perfect to be a friend; I only have to be willing to love and to serve the flawed human beings with whom God blesses me.

All that friendship requires of me is humility. Christ asks me to be humble—to know that I will never have it all together and to open the doors (to both my home and my heart) anyway. Christ himself shows me how to meet the imperfect. He wholeheartedly assures me that no one on earth will ever be perfect, and then he commands me to love them as he does.

I cannot adequately capture the incredible sense of comfort and of relief that comes when someone scoops her laundry off the couch and pulls me down into the comfort of her untidy home and her own aching heart. When we are invited into the authentic places of another woman, compassion and sympathy can flourish. When we humble ourselves to be vulnerable with one another in an effort to look to the needs of one another, Christ is there in our midst.

To be certain, there is risk. Most women will be grateful for authenticity. Some women, carefully guarding their own hearts and holding themselves to impossible standards of perfection, will cast aspersions. Because they do not know grace, they cannot extend it to someone else. If we are patient, over time, they might see the beauty and the freedom in the soft light and gentle warmth of imperfect but genuine openness to another.

Sadly, a few women never will. They cannot let their guard down long enough to be open to another woman. They cannot stop judging and finding fault long enough to see the exquisite beauty of another creature. We are left only to pray for them in the lonely fortresses they have built against friendship.

Who is the friend who speaks to your heart? Even if she exists only in your imagination, is she perfectly polished or is she tenderly authentic? Be that friend. There are women out there—many, many women—who are as hungry and eager as you are to meet that humble, compassionate soul who will enter into a real relationship where Christ's joy can be complete. Look past your own worry over your perceived shortcomings. Stop thinking about yourself. Instead, think about the person shivering on the other side of your closed door. Kick the shoes out of the way, smile from a place deep in your soul, and throw that door wide open.

Elizabeth Foss

ACTIO

 **reach out**

Invite someone in. It doesn't matter how unprepared you think you are. Brew a pot of something warm, light a candle, and call the first person God puts on your heart.

 **resolve**

How will you live out what God has shared with you in today's reading and essay?

 **rejoice**

At the end of this day, recount three blessings for which you are grateful.

1

2

3

prayer intentions

NAMES	INTENTIONS

DAILY SCRIPTURE
day seventeen

The end of all things is near; therefore be serious and discipline yourselves for the sake of your prayers. Above all, maintain constant love for one another, for love covers a multitude of sins. Be hospitable to one another without complaining. Like good stewards of the manifold grace of God, serve one another with whatever gift each of you has received. Whoever speaks must do so as one speaking the very words of God; whoever serves must do so with the strength that God supplies, so that God may be glorified in all things through Jesus Christ. To him belong the glory and the power forever and ever. Amen.

I Peter 4:7-11

for further study

Romans 12:3

lectio divina

LECTIO

1 PETER 4:7-11

In these verses, St. Peter discusses Christ's second coming, and reminds us to be vigilant in prayer and faithful to Christ's teaching. We must strive to truly love, forgive each other, and offer hospitality with a willing spirit of service. This directs us away from sin and toward being a living witness for others.

MEDITATIO

What personal message does the text have for me?

ORATIO

What do I say to the Lord in response to his word?

CONTEMPLATIO

What conversion of mind, heart, and life is he asking of me today?

How did I progress in living the word today?

In these verses, St. Peter shepherds us twenty-first century women with kind encouragement, but he doesn't mince words. He gives us rich advice about how to order our lives to bring the greatest glory to God.

The end of all things is near; therefore be serious and discipline yourselves for the sake of your prayers. (1 Peter 4:7)

Friends, I don't know about you, but I don't need reminders to check social media. My prayer life, however, requires constant redirection. If I truly lived like the end of all things were near, I'd be much more vigilant about my time.

Above all, maintain constant love for one another, for love covers a multitude of sins. (1 Peter 4:8)

Every morning I wake, determined to maintain constant love. And every day, there are moments, sometimes whole hours, when it gets crowded out by distraction, anger, jealousy, and resentment.

Constant love means constant service. It's difficult when serving seems to bring little reward. No blaring trumpets accompany a freshly changed diaper, for example. But those little acts of service, done in love, are exactly what Peter indicates will cover a multitude of sins.

Be hospitable to one another without complaining. (1 Peter 4:9)

My phone vibrated in my hand. I glanced at the screen and saw the name of a dear longtime friend.

"I'm driving through town and wanted to stop and give you a hug."

I froze and glanced around the living room. The detritus of a hundred LEGO castles littered the carpet, while my now-cold coffee sat surrounded by half-read books and dirty rocks the toddler had gifted me just this morning.

"Of course," I chirped, "I'll see you when you get here," and hung up.

Bustling out the door I hollered for the kids. For the next fifteen minutes we worked together, far from harmoniously. The kids argued with one another while I nagged. My daughter, always astute, asked, "Why do we have to do this, Mommy? Nina doesn't care if the house is clean. She told you that last time, remember?"

Yes, I remember, I thought. But I care.

My friend arrived with a hug and a smile, and after the kids had regaled her with story after silly story, I shooed them outside.

"Are you okay?" she asked. "You look flushed."

As I looked around the tidy living room, cleaned amidst tears and harsh words, it struck me that my hospitality was borne of pride rather than charity. Instead of doing my best to have a generous spirit of service, I had shown a shocking lack of charity to my own children. I had utterly failed to give hospitality without complaining.

Like good stewards of the manifold grace of God, serve one another with whatever gift each of you has received. (1 Peter 4:10)

I believe that one of the things that most pains the modern woman is the confusion between virtues and talents. Virtues inform the way we behave, while talents describe our natural aptitudes, those gifted to us by our Creator.

As Christians, we're all called to increase in the same virtues: faith, hope, charity (or love), prudence, temperance, fortitude, and justice. But as St Peter says, we must serve one another with whatever gift (talent) each of us has received.

Our culture extols talents while shunning virtue. It's more important in our society to have a good voice, for example, than it is to be a good person. In our thirst to be more talented than others—to be recognized as a better singer, writer, mother—our virtues are left by the wayside.

Loving and serving one another doesn't require talent; you don't need to be an incredible baker to invite a friend over for tea and cookies. It does require the virtue of charity, though, and, depending on how messy your home is, it may also require humility.

Talents without virtue lead to a life of vice; sinfulness and pride will fester with talent left unchecked by morality. However, when we use our talents in conjunction with the virtues of the saints, we will live the life of service that St. Peter describes.

Whoever speaks must do so as one speaking the very words of God; whoever serves must do so with the strength that God supplies, so that God may be glorified in all things through Jesus Christ. To him belong the glory and the power forever and ever. Amen. (1 Peter 4:11)

And that's really what all of this boils down to, isn't it? If our speech and our service glorify God, from whom all our talents and virtues flow, then all will be well.

Micaela Darr

ACTIO

 **reach out**

Choose one virtue to cultivate in your tasks inside and outside your home today. Set aside your striving and aim to love constantly just for today.

 **resolve**

How will you live out what God has shared with you in today's reading and essay?

 **rejoice**

At the end of this day, recount three blessings for which you are grateful.

1

2

3

prayer intentions

NAMES	INTENTIONS

DAILY SCRIPTURE
day eighteen

Let love be genuine; hate what is evil, hold fast to what is good; love one another with mutual affection; outdo one another in showing honor. Do not lag in zeal, be ardent in spirit, serve the Lord. Rejoice in hope, be patient in suffering, persevere in prayer. Contribute to the needs of the saints; extend hospitality to strangers.
Bless those who persecute you; bless and do not curse them. Rejoice with those who rejoice, weep with those who weep. Live in harmony with one another; do not be haughty, but associate with the lowly; do not claim to be wiser than you are.

Romans 12:9-16

for further study

Titus 1:8

lectio divina

LECTIO

ROMANS 12:9-16

Written by St. Paul in 57 AD, Romans is one of the most influential works in Christian history, and delves deeply into the mysteries of sin and salvation. In these verses, St. Paul discusses what constitutes a true Christian, saying that love, the greatest of all gifts, must always be used to see the good in other people. All of us have gifts that must be used to serve the Church and spread the gospel. By using these gifts and dedicating ourselves to God, our lives become a living prayer.

MEDITATIO

What personal message does the text have for me?

ORATIO

What do I say to the Lord in response to his word?

CONTEMPLATIO

What conversion of mind, heart, and life is he asking of me today?

How did I progress in living the word today?

There are a lot of people who have seen me cry. I tear up pretty regularly, and I'm really not ashamed of it. I cry when other people share their hardships with me. I get choked up when giving talks. There are even YouTube videos of me getting so worked up that my eyes start brimming with tears. I'm not ashamed of that.

Because I can control it.

Plenty of people have seen me cry just a little. I'm comfortable in that eloquent spot where I can show deep feeling without running the risk of breaking down.

Very few people have seen me sob.

But a few weeks ago, I lost it. It was at the end of Mass and I was teetering right on the edge of a breakdown, so I bit both my lips and stood silently through the closing hymn, willing myself not to start ugly crying right there.

When people started walking out, I thought I was safe. But a young woman came over and asked if she could pray with me. She'd seen that I was hurting and didn't need to know why. She just wanted to be there for me. And I cried so hard I could barely get any words out. This was the kind of crying I usually reserve for my car, the only place I'm really ever alone. I hated that I was doing it, but I couldn't help it.

And my love was accidentally genuine.

I try to be a fairly open person. I'm willing to share a lot of my struggles. I open up pretty easily when I think it will be helpful for someone else. But I rarely let myself be emotionally needy because I'm terrified of losing control, terrified of being too much.

And with the walls I put up, I rob my friends of their right to love me. I let them rejoice with me, but I don't let them weep with me. They ask how they can pray for me and I toss off something like, "Oh, just that I would be a saint," or, "You know, the usual." Because I don't want to break open my loneliness or my anger or my emptiness before them.

Not everybody has a right to those things. But I have a right to have somebody who weeps with me, somebody who rejoices in hope alongside me and stands patiently in my suffering and perseveres with me in prayer. And I can only have that kind of love if I'm willing to be genuine, not just to acknowledge the ugly parts of life from a distance, but to invite those few people to stand with me in the ugliness.

Today's passage speaks volumes about how we are to love, but it also challenges us to be loved, to take off our masks and allow other people to be Jesus to us. I've spent most of my life trying to win friendships—not to earn them, but to be the winner of each relationship. If I listen more than I talk and ask more questions and am more generous, then I win, right?

Except that friendship isn't a zero-sum game. We don't win by giving more and we don't win by taking more. The model of love that we're given as Christians is a God who was impossibly generous, even to giving up his life, while also being needy. He asked for a drink from the cross. He begged his friends to stay up praying with him. He shared the weariness of his heart and honored those who showed him great love. He was sincere and genuine, which meant being generous both in his gifts and in his needs.

When we share our suffering with people who have chosen to love us, that's not needy, that's generous. That's love. It's hard and it's scary, but it's the only love worth having.

Meg Hunter-Kilmer

ACTIO

 **reach out**

Do you have a need you've been reluctant to share with a friend today—a physical need, a care on your heart that needs a good listener, a situation you need prayer for? Reach out to a friend and invite her into that need. Risk being a friend by needing a friend.

 **resolve**

How will you live out what God has shared with you in today's reading and essay?

 **rejoice**

At the end of this day, recount three blessings for which you are grateful.

1

2

3

prayer intentions

NAMES	INTENTIONS

DAILY SCRIPTURE
day nineteen

Therefore encourage one another and build up each other, as indeed you are doing.
But we appeal to you, brothers and sisters, to respect those who labor among you, and have charge of you in the Lord and admonish you; esteem them very highly in love because of their work. Be at peace among yourselves. And we urge you, beloved, to admonish the idlers, encourage the fainthearted, help the weak, be patient with all of them. See that none of you repays evil for evil, but always seek to do good to one another and to all. Rejoice always, pray without ceasing, give thanks in all circumstances; for this is the will of God in Christ Jesus for you.

1 Thessalonians 5:11-18

for further study

Matthew 7:12

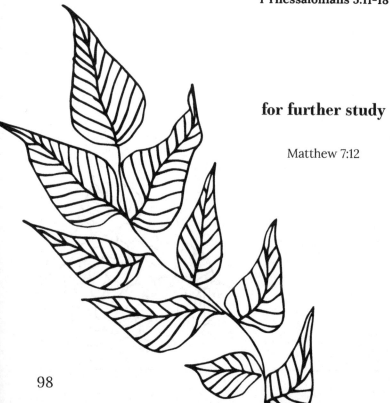

lectio divina

LECTIO

1 THESSALONIANS 5:11-18

St. Paul's first letter to the Thessalonians was written in late 50 or early 51 AD. Thessalonica, the capital of Macedonia in modern-day Greece, was largely pagan, with a small Jewish community. St. Paul won many converts, but this angered some Jews of the city, who stirred up rebellion and forced St. Paul and the other missionaries to leave. His hasty departure left the Thessalonian Christians inadequately formed and vulnerable to attacks from local detractors. In these verses, St. Paul urges Christians to live in fraternal love, work together, and pray constantly.

MEDITATIO

What personal message does the text have for me?

ORATIO

What do I say to the Lord in response to his word?

CONTEMPLATIO

What conversion of mind, heart, and life is he asking of me today?

How did I progress in living the word today?

"Mom, is this another one of your internet friends?"

When your charism is hospitality and you're a southerner, it's impossible to meet a stranger. I suppose I do have a reputation for making virtual friends into my real-life ones. As I've become active on social media, the Holy Spirit has led me to meet women through shared interests—like Cyclone basketball, the Lonestar State, or sweet tea—and experiences—a premature birth, raising a big family, or my conversion to Catholicism.

In some cases, what started out as a like, a blog comment, or a direct message, blossomed into a true, soul-filling, I-must-have-this-person-in-my-life friendship. Such is the case with my friend, Susan.

Between us, Susan and I have thirteen children. She's a Kansas farm girl and I'm a sixth-generation Texan. We have imperfect lives and we both carry heavy crosses, largely unknown to the outside world (Don't we all?). But when she and I are together, we move right past the formalities and dive deep, knowing that the other doesn't have the answers, just the ears and heart to listen. Somehow, that always ends up being enough.

I was on an anniversary vacation with my husband when my phone made the familiar "ding" announcing a text message. It said simply, "I know this is crazy, but want to help me plan an epic surprise?"

Of course, I was all in.

Susan's husband knew she needed something big for her birthday. And while the lure of jewelry or tickets to a musical were tempting, he knew she was craving a kindred spirit. Problem was that kindred spirit lived three states away. I suppose that's why they make airplanes?

When I walked in the door, she was cradling her newborn son in her arms. She was exhausted. I poked my head around the kitchen door and said, "Susan!" But before I could get the word "surprise" out of my mouth, she was on her knees in tears. All of us were, actually. Never before have I experienced such elation at seeing someone who knew my soul, and I, hers. We both needed one another.

God knows when we need the Holy Spirit's power and strength delivered to us by a friend toting chicken wings and beer, with a promise of a pedicure and college football. I'm one hundred percent sure of it. Holy and beautiful friendships with other women have opened my eyes to God's graces. His promises. His mercy. His love.

Since that birthday surprise, we have met at women's conferences and have snuck other trips in between, but we mostly rely on Voxer, text messages, sporadic phone calls, and the promise that we'll meet one another at the tabernacle each Sunday—for it's God who has his hand in our friendship. True encouragement comes from being at peace with your station in life. For when you are at peace with yourself, you can find joy in how God works in the lives of people you love.

Clearly, I believe that internet friends can become very real, very close friends. I also believe we need to be on guard for the ways the internet can thwart friendship. When you start scrolling on your phone and end up playing the comparison game, jealousy takes over. Perhaps it's time to fast from social media—for a day, a week, or longer. Invest in the things that fill your tank, so you can let that joy overflow to people you love and bask in their accomplishments, rather than letting them fuel you with discontent. Connect with the friend right in front of you. She needs your presence, your encouragement, and your undivided attention.

Then, you can return to social media with fresh perspective, able to discern the places where he is calling you into the joy of genuine friends. Each time Susan and I say goodbye, the hug is a little tighter, the tears fall a little quicker, but the gratitude grows bigger. There is comfort and strength in knowing that I do not walk this journey of motherhood alone. My heart is full. God doesn't promise us an easy life, easy deliveries, easy marriages, easy kids, or easy crosses, but he does promise us eternity and the friends who will travel there with us.

Kathryn Whitaker

ACTIO

 **reach out**

Today, let's think about internet friends. How can you deepen a friendship that has begun online; how can you give it more fullness and bring it more completely into your "real" life?

 **resolve**

How will you live out what God has shared with you in today's reading and essay?

 **rejoice**

At the end of this day, recount three blessings for which you are grateful.

1

2

3

prayer intentions

NAMES	INTENTIONS

DAILY SCRIPTURE
day twenty

Love is patient; love is kind; love is not envious or boastful or arrogant or rude. It does not insist on its own way; it is not irritable or resentful; it does not rejoice in wrongdoing, but rejoices in the truth. It bears all things, believes all things, hopes all things, endures all things.

1 Corinthians 13:4-7

for further study

1 John 2:10

lectio divina

LECTIO

1 CORINTHIANS 13:4-7

St. Paul wrote to the church in Corinth around 56 AD, five years after the church was founded. In that time, the church has been fraught with division and doctrinal confusion. Therefore, the letter was written to address these problems and bring about unity and resolution. Today's verses discuss how Christian faith and good citizenship go together and should never be opposed to one another. We are obligated to live in obedience with the civil law, so long as it is just.

MEDITATIO

What personal message does the text have for me?

ORATIO

What do I say to the Lord in response to his word?

CONTEMPLATIO

What conversion of mind, heart, and life is he asking of me today?

How did I progress in living the word today?

The summer before I started sixth grade, my family went camping with a group of friends. I spent a good chunk of the trip away from everyone else with my book in my camping chair, tears streaming down my face, fearing summer's end and the beginning of middle school. But guess what, guys: this anxious preteen made it out. I beat the middle school monster.

As an adult, it would be difficult for me to have patience with eleven-year-old me and her ridiculous fear of the school day. But instead of telling me that there was nothing to worry about, my father considered my anxiety from my perspective. He knew my stressed-out little mind needed rest and I couldn't sleep. On tearful nights he would tell me a rhyme, sometimes rubbing my back, to try and stop my thoughts from racing. Part of it said, "Think of ponds, still and deep. Think of bunnies, fast asleep." And I would imagine a quiet pond at dusk, with summertime crickets chirping. And near the pond, I would think about baby rabbits with their ears back and eyes closed, their little bodies moving up and down with each sleepy breath. And the imaginary rhythm of their breathing would calm my own, and I'd tell myself I'd be just fine, just fine, just fine.

Love is patient; love is kind; love is not envious or boastful or arrogant or rude.

Someone once described the difference between sympathy and empathy to me as a man stuck in hole. A friend walks past the dude in the hole and says, "Dang, man. How'd you get yourself down there? That sucks. I'm so sorry. You got help?" And the guy in the hole replies, "Yeah, just called for a ladder. Thanks for asking." A little while later, a second friend comes by and she says, "Dang! You're in a tight spot!" and she goes down to join him in the hole until the ladder comes.

It's not a perfect analogy. You can never truly join the friend in the hole. Despite what Atticus Finch claims, another person's shoes will never fit our own feet perfectly, no matter how far we walk in them. But we can try. And I'm very bad at this part: trying doesn't look like solving their problems.

Usually, you can't bring the ladder, solve the anxiety, or mend the heart. They have to do it themselves. But maybe you can bring down a flashlight or a snack and spend some time in the hole with her to make it seem a little less daunting.

Love does not insist on its own way; it is not irritable or resentful; it does not rejoice in wrongdoing, but rejoices in the truth.

Climbing into the hole with a friend isn't difficult to attempt if a friend's struggle is objectively challenging. But I find it hardest to love well when I don't think that a friend's problems are all that tough.

But the time to show the most love is when it might seem okay to "slack off." No one would have blamed adult Dad for telling anxious, preteen me to just "calm down." But I felt more love when Dad joined me in the hole of my anxiety. He did what he could to help me face the next few seconds, or minutes, or days, and eventually I got myself out. That's what true patience looks like.

Sometimes my friends and family make choices I wish they didn't. That is when love is truly a test. But I'm my best self when I take them with all their fears and sins, and say, "I'm here with you." So much of the work of sincere love is choosing to engage when everyone else would not judge us for backing off. So much of love is simply, sincerely showing up.

Love bears all things, believes all things, hopes all things, endures all things.

All things. We will survive this. We can help our friends survive this. All we need is love.

Katy Greiner

ACTIO

 **reach out**

Think of a friend who finds herself in a hole in her life right now. Find one small way you can "enter in" to that hole with her and hold out the light of love.

 **resolve**

How will you live out what God has shared with you in today's reading and essay?

 **rejoice**

At the end of this day, recount three blessings for which you are grateful.

1

2

3

prayer intentions

NAMES	INTENTIONS

day twenty-one

Selah is a Hebrew word found often in the psalms and a few times in Habakkuk. Scholars aren't absolutely certain what it means. It seems to be a musical or liturgical note—maybe a pause or maybe a crescendo.

We have set aside this space—this day—for you to use as your selah. Perhaps you pause here and just review what you have pondered thus far. Perhaps you rejoice here and use the space for shouts of praise. Or maybe you take the opportunity to fill in some gaps in the pages before this one.

It's your space. Selah. Give it meaning.

scripture
MEMORY
week four
day twenty-two

This week we have a pretty hefty chunk of Scripture for you, but as you leave this study, we want you to be fully equipped to go out into the world and be a true friend. This one might take you a little longer than a week. Divide it up and work on it over time. You'll be so glad you did.

Finally, be strong in the Lord and in the strength of his power. Put on the whole armor of God, so that you may be able to stand against the wiles of the devil. For our struggle is not against enemies of blood and flesh, but against the rulers, against the authorities, against the cosmic powers of this present darkness, against the spiritual forces of evil in the heavenly places. Therefore take up the whole armor of God, so that you may be able to withstand on that evil day, and having done everything, to stand firm. Stand therefore, and fasten the belt of truth around your waist, and put on the breastplate of righteousness. As shoes for your feet put on whatever will make you ready to proclaim the gospel of peace. With all of these, take the shield of faith, with which you will be able to quench all the flaming arrows of the evil one. Take the helmet of salvation, and the sword of the Spirit, which is the word of God. Pray in the Spirit at all times in every prayer and supplication. To that end keep alert and always persevere in supplication for all the saints.

EPHESIANS 6:10-18

EPHESIANS 6:16

DAILY SCRIPTURE
day twenty-three

After Jesus had spoken these words, he went out with his disciples across the Kidron valley to a place where there was a garden, which he and his disciples entered. Now Judas, who betrayed him, also knew the place, because Jesus often met there with his disciples. So Judas brought a detachment of soldiers together with police from the chief priests and the Pharisees, and they came there with lanterns and torches and weapons.

John 18:1-3

Well meant are the wounds a friend inflicts,
but profuse are the kisses of an enemy.

Proverbs 27:6

lectio divina

LECTIO

JOHN 18:1-3

St. John wrote his Gospel before 100 AD with the intent to convince people that Jesus is the Christ, the Son of God (20:31). In these verses, Jesus takes his friends into the Garden of Gethsemane, in the Kidron Valley, where Judas will meet him with a band of guards and soldiers.

MEDITATIO

What personal message does the text have for me?

ORATIO

What do I say to the Lord in response to his word?

CONTEMPLATIO

What conversion of mind, heart, and life is he asking of me today?

How did I progress in living the word today?

I was raised in a nominally Catholic home and came to a conversion experience in early adulthood. Here's a thing that really surprised me about the Church, the thing that took a couple of decades to reconcile in my own mind: the real, authentic Church of God himself is full of sinners who hurt one another. Sometimes, they even hurt one another in the name of Christ (however mistaken they might be). Further, I am a sinner, and, as much as I hope not to, I hurt people sometimes, too. Hurt happens. Even in the Church. Maybe especially in the Church.

We expect so much more of one another. We assume that every interaction will happen with the grace and peace of God. And then it doesn't. And we are mightily confused and utterly bewildered because we thought that Christians were just like Jesus. The truth is that Christians are just like the sinners who sat with Jesus in the Upper Room. They can deny a friendship if it is expedient to do so. They can betray a trust if a seemingly better opportunity presents itself. They can jockey for social position with a group of tightly-knit friends, and for standing in the community outside that group.

God knew this would happen. He knew that that girl who said she loved you would betray you with a kiss. He knew that she would couch her words with disclaimers like "maternal correction" so that they would sound holy, but that really they were kisses of an enemy. Jesus even knew that it would take you a while to sift the grain from the chaff, to understand whose words are the things necessary for true growth and whose were not uttered in charity at all.

He knew and he went before you so that you could turn, weeping, and rest in his arms and you'd be certain that when he said he understood, he really did. He knows how it feels when you look into the eyes of someone you loved well, and she returns your gaze with a look of contempt, or of mocking laughter, or of unbridled rage, or of embarrassed shame at the sell-out she has plotted and executed. He knows because he saw those eyes in the flesh and he felt that pain with his own beating heart.

He can console you and comfort you and breathe life back into you when you've been crushed by a friendship's painful end. And he will—every time you ask him into the pain.

But as I think of those times in my life when I've been hurt by a friend, the thing that strikes me now, many years later and with the grace of having come to a place of peace, is that one of the strong themes of this book is being the friend we want to have. And so, one of the admonitions of this week's study has to be to look at myself and see all the ways I've failed at friendship, all the times that my actions have more closely resembled Judas in the garden or Peter before the cock crowed. I think it's important to take some time with these verses and ask honestly if we have failed at friendship because we've been more like Judas than we've previously considered possible.

Judas used Jesus for his own gain. He sold out a friendship for his own selfish interests. He valued his own ambitions and desires more than he valued the treasure that was friendship with the Lord.

I can't honestly say that I've never committed that sin.

Can you?

Elizabeth Foss

ACTIO

 **reach out**

Ask forgiveness today of someone you have betrayed in a big or small way. If it is not appropriate to reach out personally at this time, ask for that forgiveness in prayer. Consider whether the friend whose forgiveness you need might be yourself or the Lord.

 **resolve**

How will you live out what God has shared with you in today's reading and essay?

 **rejoice**

At the end of this day, recount three blessings for which you are grateful.

1

2

3

prayer intentions

NAMES	INTENTIONS

DAILY SCRIPTURE
day twenty-four

When they had finished breakfast, Jesus said to Simon Peter, "Simon son of John, do you love me more than these?" He said to him, "Yes, Lord; you know that I love you." Jesus said to him, "Feed my lambs." A second time he said to him, "Simon son of John, do you love me?" He said to him, "Yes, Lord; you know that I love you." Jesus said to him, "Tend my sheep."

John 21:15-16

for further study

1 Corinthians 5:18-19

lectio divina

LECTIO

JOHN 21:15-16

St. John's Gospel is the most theologically rich of all the gospels, and was called the "spiritual gospel" in the early church. In today's verses, St. John gives us Peter's repudiation of his betrayal of Jesus, replacing his earlier statements with three professions of love. Jesus asks Peter to love the Church that he will leave in Peter's keeping.

MEDITATIO

What personal message does the text have for me?

ORATIO

What do I say to the Lord in response to his word?

CONTEMPLATIO

What conversion of mind, heart, and life is he asking of me today?

How did I progress in living the word today?

A punch to the gut. That's what it felt like.

I stared at my phone in disbelief. Did the text message from my friend say what I thought it said? I closed my eyes and shook my head a few times, hoping that, with those movements, the text would disappear, or change, or something, anything to remove the knife that was slowly twisting in my heart. Yet when I opened my eyes and looked again, they were still there: those awful, heart-wrenching words that cut me to the core.

Reeling, I pounded out my response and quickly hit send; I had to know what she meant. Texting with my friend, while convenient, didn't allow for the nuances of tone and other non-verbal cues. I probably should have just called her and cleared everything up right then, but I didn't.

After a dozen more texts were exchanged, I typed, "I forgive you, but it's going to take me a while to process what just happened. I hope you and your family have a wonderful Christmas, and hopefully I'll talk to you in the new year." And then I turned off my phone and wept.

Weeks, then months passed. I thought about calling my friend nearly every day, but something—my wounded pride? Residual anger? Fear of rejection?—stopped me. It was so foreign, the canyon of silence that separated us. We'd been thick as thieves for years, rarely allowing a day to go by without checking in or catching up.

When our family relocated 2,500 miles from home, I didn't know a soul. It was this woman who had created a sacred spot for me, both in her home and in her heart. We spent hours talking about life, faith, and family. And oh, how we laughed. I once told her that if the only good that came from being uprooted from my former life was meeting her, it would have all been worth it. I finally found the kindred-est of kindred spirits, a forever friend.

And now, where once was unconditional love and mutual support, there was weighty silence and grief.
After much soul searching, I finally realized that, while hurtful, my friend's words held a kernel of pointed truth about a particularly difficult situation in my life. But... how could we make it past the hurt feelings between us?

Scripture shows us that Jesus didn't shy away from intimacy. He was familiar with the nitty-gritty of close relationships. Peter's betrayal on Holy Thursday must have hurt him deeply, and yet our Lord didn't hold it against him. Jesus offered Peter the opportunity to repent, and Peter rose to the occasion, reconciling with the Lord. I find it interesting that Jesus didn't approach Peter until after breakfast—once they'd been at table together, and their bellies were full. Indeed, how much easier would my friend's words been received had we been sitting on her back porch drinking a cup of coffee rather than trying to interpret the meaning and motive of texted words?

It was painful to admit I had been wrong. Even more painful, though, was the thought of losing the very best friend I'd ever had because I didn't have the guts to apologize. In 2 Corinthians 5:18, Saint Paul tells us that Christ "gave us the *ministry* of reconciliation." (emphasis mine) By failing to make amends with my friend, I was rejecting our Lord's gift. I also knew that sometimes ministry, like love, wasn't always lollipops and rainbows.

One sunny afternoon, I swallowed my pride and dialed her number. "Hi," I said. "I'm so sorry it took me this long to call. I'm praying that you will please, please forgive my hardness of heart. I am so sorry for hurting you. Friend, will you forgive me?" And you know what? She forgave me on the spot. She apologized again to me for her words, and I forgave her on the spot, too. Pretty soon, we were laughing and crying at the same time, because that's what dear friends do when, by the grace of God, the heavy chains of sin and pride are broken and the fragrant aroma of reconciliation blooms anew.

Heather Renshaw

ACTIO

 **reach out**

Is there someone in your life to whom you need extend an invitation to reconnect after a period of distance, for whatever reason? Extend that invitation today, forgiving yourself for not doing it sooner, and praying that her heart will be open.

 **resolve**

How will you live out what God has shared with you in today's reading and essay?

 **rejoice**

At the end of this day, recount three blessings for which you are grateful.

1

2

3

prayer intentions

NAMES	INTENTIONS

DAILY SCRIPTURE
day twenty-five

After some days Paul said to Barnabas, "Come, let us return and visit the believers in every city where we proclaimed the word of the Lord and see how they are doing." Barnabas wanted to take with them John called Mark. But Paul decided not to take with them one who had deserted them in Pamphylia and had not accompanied them in the work. The disagreement became so sharp that they parted company; Barnabas took Mark with him and sailed away to Cyprus. But Paul chose Silas and set out, the believers commending him to the grace of the Lord. He went through Syria and Cilicia, strengthening the churches.

Acts 15:36-41

for further study

2 Corinthians 4:16-18

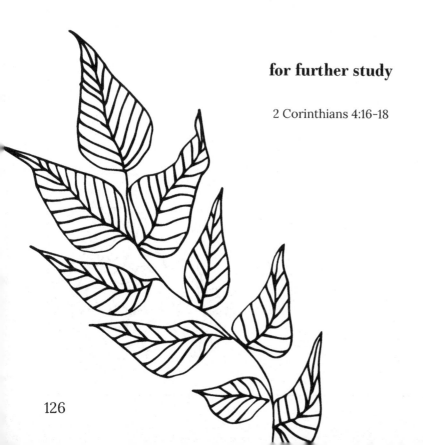

lectio divina

LECTIO

ACTS 15:36-41

Written by St. Luke around 63 AD, Acts recounts the growth of the early Church, in Jerusalem and throughout the wider world. But even though the Holy Spirit guides the growth of the Church, it doesn't stop arguments and dissension from happening, as we see in today's verses. St. Paul and his friend Barnabas have an argument over the role of John Mark, a fellow disciple, and it's strong enough to sever their relationship.

MEDITATIO

What personal message does the text have for me?

ORATIO

What do I say to the Lord in response to his word?

CONTEMPLATIO

What conversion of mind, heart, and life is he asking of me today?

How did I progress in living the word today?

When we look at Barnabas and Paul's relationship we see one of encouragement and mentorship. Barnabas means "son of encouragement," and if it weren't for his personal spiritual investment in Paul, we might never have been blessed with this powerhouse preaching team. It was Barnabas who vouched for Paul with the apostles, and it was Barnabas who taught Paul how to preach to the early Church. These men did amazing things together until they had a disagreement about Mark, another disciple of Christ.

This disagreement was so intense, they decided to go their separate ways. Barnabas and Mark literally "sailed away," a decision that had to be difficult for everyone.

Can you imagine the devastation they must have felt? Walking away from a friendship based on mutual trust and a common goal, with shared memories and experiences that no one else understood but Paul and Barnabas. Yet, despite the emotional pain, the men continued—separately—to spread the gospel as God instructed them.

I have experienced the loss of a friendship or two over the course of my lifetime. One in particular remains a bruise on my heart. I had known this woman for some time and we had shared much over the course of our relationship. I trusted her with my troubles and she trusted me with hers in return. We celebrated sweet victories, and we buoyed each other up after occasional setbacks. We always had fun together.

Our disagreement came over a situation involving a mutual friend. Much like Paul and Barnabas, we could not come to an agreement on how things should be handled. Our last conversation took place over text messages with accusations made and hurt feelings expressed. I called repeatedly, knowing there had to be a better way to discuss this issue, but she refused my calls. I was left deeply wounded and really confused as to why we could not just "agree to disagree" and move on.

Our parting was very unexpected and I still carry the scar. It

has led me to question the loyalty of my other friendships, and to be very careful about with whom I share my life. I hate that I'm still wary of certain people, but I know that God is healing the wound left by that relationship rupture through the sisterly love of other women he has brought to my life.

It's never a pleasant realization that, no matter how hard you try, a friendship cannot be salvaged, and you are forced to see there is no going back. How do we handle that pain with grace, so we can set one another free from the obligation of a friendship that is no longer working, and bless each other as we move forward on our own journeys?

For me, it comes down to two simple practices: humility and prayer. I did my best. I humbly reached out several times to try and fix things and finally, through prayer and the counsel of my spiritual director, I found peace by letting that friendship go.

I maintain my peace by praying for my sister in Christ and asking for forgiveness for any hurt I may have caused in the parting. I wish her no ill will and I do not think poorly of her when she comes up in conversations with other mutual friends. I live my life fully and no longer let the relationship dominate my thoughts.

I imagine that Paul and Barnabas did the same for each other. After all, they were brothers in Christ. What is established in faith doesn't fall away so easily.

If you are facing the end of a friendship, I encourage you to take it to prayer and ask God the Father into your hurt and your pain, allowing him to heal you. Regardless of whether your friend will engage in the conversation of forgiveness, bring your friend before the throne of God as well. Even though your friendship might be over, you are still sisters in Christ, and it is in forgiving and moving forward—no matter whether she acknowledges your forgiveness or reciprocates—that you will continue your own spiritual journey in the peace of Christ.

Mary Lenaburg

ACTIO

 **reach out**

Pray a prayer of surrender and closure for a friendship you've had to let go of in your life. Offer the joys, works, and sufferings of your day freely for that person's well-being.

 **resolve**

How will you live out what God has shared with you in today's reading and essay?

 **rejoice**

At the end of this day, recount three blessings for which you are grateful.

1

2

3

prayer intentions

NAMES	INTENTIONS

DAILY SCRIPTURE
day twenty-six

One day, while he was teaching, Pharisees and teachers of the law were sitting near by (they had come from every village of Galilee and Judea and from Jerusalem); and the power of the Lord was with him to heal. Just then some men came, carrying a paralyzed man on a bed. They were trying to bring him in and lay him before Jesus; but finding no way to bring him in because of the crowd, they went up on the roof and let him down with his bed through the tiles into the middle of the crowd in front of Jesus. When he saw their faith, he said, "Friend, your sins are forgiven you." Then the scribes and the Pharisees began to question, "Who is this who is speaking blasphemies? Who can forgive sins but God alone?" When Jesus perceived their questionings, he answered them, "Why do you raise such questions in your hearts? Which is easier, to say, 'Your sins are forgiven you,' or to say, 'Stand up and walk'? But so that you may know that the Son of Man has authority on earth to forgive sins"—he said to the one who was paralyzed—"I say to you, stand up and take your bed and go to your home." Immediately he stood up before them, took what he had been lying on, and went to his home, glorifying God. Amazement seized all of them, and they glorified God and were filled with awe, saying, "We have seen strange things today."

Luke 5:17-26

for further study

Proverbs 17:17

lectio divina

LECTIO

LUKE 5:17-26

The theme of St. Luke's Gospel is the universality of the good news—Jesus comes to save everyone from sin and death. While Jesus heals people physically, that is never all he does; he always heals them of their sins as well. Such is the case in today's story of the healing of the paralytic. However, the paralytic man would never have reached Jesus without the assistance and devotion of his friends.

MEDITATIO

What personal message does the text have for me?

ORATIO

What do I say to the Lord in response to his word?

CONTEMPLATIO

What conversion of mind, heart, and life is he asking of me today?

How did I progress in living the word today?

I have been navigating a crisis situation in my life for a few months now. It is painful and often paralyzing. It has made me distrustful and doubtful on many occasions. I repeat far too often that I cannot do this any longer, that I am just too tired. Like the man in this gospel, my pain and weakness take over, and I lie down on my mat, unsure how to get myself to the great healer, certain that I do not have the strength.

And without fail, they begin to arrive. One by one, sometimes in pairs, come the friends, the intimate circle of people whom I have let see this creeping, aching woundedness in my soul. They come in text messages and phone calls if they are far away. They come to the door with deliveries of household necessities and to the café across the street for breakfast. They come in the form of understanding and compassionate social workers and therapists. They show up, and without their knowledge, they fuse together in a team that moves in unison. And as one, they lift me, they carry me, they take me to where my Lord is, believing he can make me strong again.

It is not without cost and great effort on their part. I am heavy with the weight of this pain sometimes. Jesus feels far away and inaccessible and I do not always make it easy to carry me. My friends take risks to help me, and they have been maligned and pushed out of the way by people who would keep me from him. It is a long haul to that rooftop with me in tow.

And it's not easy for me either. Friendship is hard for me. Lately, I have been hurt often. My instinct is to trust people only so far, to pretend I don't need them, and then to coil away in shame when I do. I am always afraid of becoming too much for people, too heavy a burden to carry. I am apologetic about needing them. Sometimes I even thrash about when they bend to lift me, and I feel my control ebbing away. I don't like not being able to see where I am being carried, when my mat wobbles and sways and I can't still the motion, when I am tipped and dipped on the way to the roof. I have full faith that the only place these friends would carry me is to the arms of Christ; my fear is not where I'll end up in their hands. My fear is of how I might suffer in the carrying.

And yet there is no denying that I need to be at the feet of Christ, and that my paralysis prevents me from getting there. Often enough, I make the choice to lie very still on that mat. So the question to my heart becomes this: if I am willing to trust Jesus' power to heal me, am I not willing to trust the people and the process he has put into place to get me to him when I cannot get myself there? If people are willing to risk offering their friendship and loving me with such depth that they would take on this arduous task of bearing my weight in order to see to my healing, is not my calling as a follower of Christ to be a friend in return, by offering them genuine humility and sincere gratitude? And by giving them the trust they most certainly have earned?

Looking back at my own experiences of reaching out as a friend, I know how much intimacy is built when I offer to enter in to someone's hard place and listen as she opens her heart to me. I am deeply grateful for the friendships in my life where that experience is part of our shared history. There is deep and wide grace in allowing a friend to carry you to Jesus, humblingly aware that you need him desperately. Because in the end, you both end up at his feet, begging he heal you both. Together.

Colleen Mitchell

ACTIO

 **reach out**

Trust. Who has betrayed your trust? In whom do you trust? How can you reconcile wariness born of hard experiences and the call to open to friends who can and will carry you to the foot of the cross?

 **resolve**

How will you live out what God has shared with you in today's reading and essay?

 **rejoice**

At the end of this day, recount three blessings for which you are grateful.

1

2

3

prayer intentions

NAMES	INTENTIONS

DAILY SCRIPTURE
day twenty-seven

Therefore, since we are surrounded by so great a cloud of witnesses, let us also lay aside every weight and the sin that clings so closely, and let us run with perseverance the race that is set before us, looking to Jesus the pioneer and perfecter of our faith, who for the sake of the joy that was set before him endured the cross, disregarding its shame, and has taken his seat at the right hand of the throne of God. Consider him who endured such hostility against himself from sinners, so that you may not grow weary or lose heart.

Hebrews 12:1-3

for further study

Job 16:20-21

lectio divina

LECTIO

HEBREWS 12:1-3

The author of Hebrews places Christ as the "pioneer and perfecter of our faith," a theme that is echoed in today's verses. Christ is the ultimate example of patience and fidelity to God's will. In our lives, suffering is inevitable, as are temptations and difficulties, but with prayer, discipline, and the grace of Christ, we can overcome these obstacles and grow in holiness. The saints are our examples, inspiring and motivating us to live the full Christian life.

MEDITATIO

What personal message does the text have for me?

ORATIO

What do I say to the Lord in response to his word?

CONTEMPLATIO

What conversion of mind, heart, and life is he asking of me today?

How did I progress in living the word today?

When I was single, I lived for a year with friends. Several months after moving into our condo, we decided to throw a little housewarming party. (Because who would pass up an opportunity for a party?)

During the gathering, a young man invited by a roommate walked past our bookshelves (really, they were mine) and glanced up at a framed photo there.

"Whose picture is this?" he asked. "It belongs to me," I answered. "He's an old friend."

As soon as the words spilled out of my mouth, the young man responded, "Oh, really? He's my old friend too." Yes, we both referred to him in the same way.

This photo was a picture of St. Josemaría Escrivá. I had "met" him when I was sixteen, on a pilgrimage to Rome in 2000 for World Youth Day. One day, we stopped in the church where he is buried on the Via Buozzi, just outside the walls of Rome, to celebrate Mass over his relics.

Somehow that day and the remaining weeks of summer found me beginning to be captivated by this saint. His snippets of wisdom were just the thing to draw my heart back to Christ when I felt myself adrift during my teenage years. His spirituality drew me to connect with other wonderful women also looking to live their life in Christ, to make their work a prayer. I found purpose in the Lord even in mundane tasks through St. Josemaría's inspiration.

But further, I always found him to have a listening ear when I was having "guy troubles," or struggling to know my vocation. My first breakup in high school, around the time I was seventeen, had me on my knees asking for the intercession of St. Josemaría in healing from the heartache, pleading for clarity in knowing my vocation. (That was not the last time that exact same prayer was poured out.)

Fast forward to this young man who also calls St. Josemaría his old friend... We spent hours chatting that evening after

being introduced by our mutual heavenly friend. Several months passed getting to know each other, then we became husband and wife. On our honeymoon, we went back to that church in Rome on the Via Buozzi and attended Mass once again over the tomb of our old friend, carrying prayers of thanksgiving for bringing us together. On our second anniversary, we discovered we were expecting our second girl, who was due to be born on his feast day. She carries the middle name Marie in his honor. Our old friend continues to be a family intercessor.

Friendship with the saints is powerful. The "cloud of witnesses" referred to in the twelfth chapter of Hebrews is the Church Triumphant—our heavenly friends, the saints. Without ceasing, they behold the face of God. And they desire nothing more than to point us to Christ, to help us follow the will of God in our lives.

> In the lives of those who, sharing in our humanity are, however, more perfectly transformed into the image of Christ, God vividly manifests his presence and his face to men. He speaks to us in them, and gives us a sign of his kingdom to which we are strongly drawn. ... For just as Christian communion among wayfarers brings us closer to Christ, so our companionship with the saints joins us to Christ. (*Lumen Gentium* 50)

As with our earthly friendships, a heavenly friend may follow us for life. Other times, it is just for a season. But whatever the duration, it is good to have them by our side as we navigate this temporal pilgrimage. Their friendship is a great gift given by the Lord that we shouldn't be afraid to benefit from whenever we are in need of comfort, aid, or any other material or spiritual care.

May you, too, find cherished companionship with heavenly friends!

Laurel Muff

ACTIO

 **reach out**

Think about a particular saint or biblical figure who has been a friend to you in a difficult time. Share that story with someone in your life who might need that kind of encouragement today.

 **resolve**

How will you live out what God has shared with you in today's reading and essay?

 **rejoice**

At the end of this day, recount three blessings for which you are grateful.

1

2

3

prayer intentions

NAMES	INTENTIONS

day twenty-eight

Selah is a Hebrew word found often in the psalms and a few times in Habakkuk. Scholars aren't absolutely certain what it means. It seems to be a musical or liturgical note—maybe a pause or maybe a crescendo.

We have set aside this space—this day—for you to use as your selah. Perhaps you pause here and just review what you have pondered thus far. Perhaps you rejoice here and use the space for shouts of praise. Or maybe you take the opportunity to fill in some gaps in the pages before this one.

It's your space. Selah. Give it meaning.

WHY LECTIO DIVINA?

Together, as a community of faithful women, we endeavor to better understand the heart of the gospel and to live it out in our lives. Each day, we invite our souls to encounter our Lord.

How? How will the tired soul living in the woman in the midst of secular culture and busyness still herself and find her Lord? How will she find hope and new energy in the act of one more thing on her to-do list?

She will pray—more. That's right. She will take more time to pray even though so many things pull on her time. Can we do that together? Can we take up for ourselves the ancient tradition of lectio divina and let the Word lead us to live in charity? We can and we must. This is the best way to prepare ourselves for each day with peaceful composure and serene grace.

In his 2010 apostolic exhortation *Verbum Domini*, Pope Benedict XVI beautifully instructs the faithful to prayerfully read the Scripture. Following his lead, we will be drawn into a practice that is as old as Scripture itself. We will closely read and ponder Scripture passages carefully chosen for this season.

In the early Christian communities, Scripture was read to nourish faith with the wisdom of truth. When we hold the New Testament, we take up the understanding that the first Christians had of the Old Testament, together with the divine revelation the Holy Spirit granted to Jesus' earliest followers.

The Church Fathers' faith was informed by their careful, prayerful reading of the word. Today, we are blessed to welcome their wisdom into our reading when we access the commentaries that were the fruit of their lectio. The monastic movement grew in the fertile soil of lectio divina. The daily, ordered life of the monks was (and is) centered upon spiritual reading of Scripture. Can ordinary women in the twenty-first century find spiritual nourishment and new life in this age-old practice of holy men?

We can.

There are five steps in the pattern, five distinct movements that will direct the way we travel through our days. First, we read. Then, a meditation engages the mind, using reason to search for knowledge in the message. The prayer is the movement of the heart towards God, a beseeching on behalf of the soul. The contemplation elevates the mind and suspends it in God's presence. Finally, the action is the way we live our lives as a gift of charity towards others. It's a tall order, but it's the very best way to live.

Let's take a careful look at each step.

Pope Benedict writes, "It opens with the reading (*lectio*) of a text, which leads to a desire to understand its true content: what does the biblical text say in itself." (*Verbum Domini*, 87) This is where we explore the literary genre of the text, the characters we meet in the story, and the objective meaning intended by the author. We usually offer several passages which work together towards a common theme; you can choose just one passage, or you can look at the group together, as the Holy Spirit inspires. A good study Bible and/or a Bible dictionary will help you to place the reading in context.

"Next comes meditation (*meditatio*), which asks: what does the biblical text say to us?" (DV, 87) Prayerfully we ponder what personal message the text holds for each of us and what effect that message should have on our lives.

"Following this comes prayer (*oratio*), which asks the question: what do we say to the Lord in response to his word? Prayer, as petition, intercession, thanksgiving and praise, is the primary way by which the word transforms us." (DV, 87) What do we say to God in response to his Word? We ask him what he desires of us. We ask him for the strength and grace to do his will. Moved by his mercy, we give him thanks and praise.

The fourth act is "contemplation (*contemplatio*), during which we take up, as a gift from God, his own way of seeing and judging reality, and ask ourselves what conversion of mind, heart and life is the Lord asking of us?" (DV, 87) Here, reflect on how God has conveyed his love for us in the day's Scripture. Recognize the beauty of his gifts and the goodness of his mercy and rest in that. Let God light you from within and look out on the world in a new way because you have been transformed by the process of prayerful Scripture study.

Finally, the whole point of this time we've taken from our day is to get up from the reading and go live the gospel. Actio is where we make an act of our wills and resolve to bring the text to life in our lives.

This is our fiat.

> The process of lectio divina is not concluded until it arrives at action (*actio*), which moves the believer to make his or her life a gift for others in charity. We find the supreme synthesis and fulfillment of this process in the Mother of God. For every member of the faithful Mary is the model of docile acceptance of God's word, for she "kept all these things, pondering them in her heart." (Lk 2:19; cf. 2:51) (DV, 87)

As a community at Take Up & Read, we will endeavor to engage in lectio divina every day. To correlate with each day's Scripture passages, we've created pages for your time of prayer, and we've created pages for your active time. We want this book to come alive in your hands, to bring you a spiritual springtime. Try to take the time each day to dig deep, but if you have to cut your time short, don't be discouraged. Ask the Blessed Mother to help you find pockets throughout the day to re-engage. You don't have to fill in every box. There is no right or wrong answer. And you don't have to dig deeply with every passage.

Pray the parts you can, and trust the Holy Spirit to water it well in your soul. Know that God can do loaves and fishes miracles with your small parcels of time, if only you are willing to offer him what you have. Before your days—and then your weeks—get swallowed with the ordinary to-do lists of life's hustle, sit in prayer and see how you can tune your heart to the beat of the Lord's, and ensure that the best gift you give is your life, poured out for others in charity.

MEET THE AUTHORS

Micaela Darr lives in Southern California and is a happy wife to her husband, and mother to seven charming kiddos, age twelve down to newborn. In her former life, she was an elementary and middle school teacher outside the home. Now, as a homeschooling mom, she does both those jobs (and many more) for far less money, but also more joy. She renewed her love of writing by starting a blog when her family took a two year adventure to South Korea, and has since contributed her writing to several other Catholic websites, and has two books set to be published in 2018. Her latest out-of-the-home adventure is planning a small Catholic women's conference that aims to strengthen women on their journey to be closer to the God who loves them.

Emily DeArdo is a lifelong Ohioan and inveterate bibliophile. When she's not reading, writing, or editing, Emily can be found re-reading Jane Austen, knitting, trying out new recipes, cheering for the Pittsburgh Penguins, drinking tea, or enjoying a meal with friends. Her first book, *Catholic 101*, was released in 2017, and she's currently working on a memoir about faith and life after a double-lung transplant. To follow her adventures, visit her on Instagram at @emily_deardo or at emilymdeardo.com

Elizabeth Foss spends her days (and some nights) seeking beauty and truth and then searching for just the right words to express what she's found. The Founder and Content Director of Take Up & Read, she's astonished and incredibly grateful to have the opportunity to do work she loves with people she loves. Elizabeth lives in Loudoun County, Virginia with her husband and six of her nine kids, but frequently travels south to Charlottesville and north to New York and Connecticut to work (and play) with her grown children.

Katy Greiner is a freshly minted high school English teacher who's seeking peace amidst the healthy chaos change brings. When she's not looking over her shoulder for the real adult in the room to take care of her freshmen, she's planning trips or craving Chick-Fil-A. She loves a good sunset, great conversations, a strong cup of tea, all kinds of music, and hearing God laugh.

Ana Hahn is a wife of nine years and mother of five. She enjoys educating her three school-aged daughters at home and playing planes with her two toddler boys. In her rare spare time she works on making her home bright and cheerful and sharing bits of that, as well as other motherhood musings, on her blog, Time Flies When You're Having Babies.

Meg Hunter-Kilmer is a hobo missionary. After earning two theology degrees from Notre Dame and spending five years as a high school religion teacher, she quit her job in 2012 to live out of her car and preach the Gospel to anyone who would listen. Fifty states and twenty countries later, this seems to have been a less ridiculous decision than she initially thought. She blogs at www.piercedhands.com and at www.aleteia.org, though she's much more prolific on Instagram and Facebook.

Mary Lenaburg is a writer, speaker, wife, and mother who travels around the country sharing her testimony about God's redeeming love and being brave in the scared. Mary currently works at Tepeyac OB-GYN, a pro-life medical practice near her home in Northern Virginia. She lives with her husband of twenty-nine years and her son and continues to embrace her father's advice: "Never quit, never give up, never lose your faith. It's the one reason you walk this earth. For God chose this time and place just for you, so make the most of it."

Rakhi McCormick is a wife and mother who works in parish communications part-time while trying to keep up with her husband, three young children, and a growing creative business in Metro Detroit. She is a first-generation Indian-American and a convert from Hinduism. Rakhi has a passion for sharing the encouraging good news of the Gospel. When not chasing her children, you can find her writing, singing, dreaming of Italy, hanging out on Instagram (@rakstardesigns), and making beautiful things, all with coffee in hand. Some of her creative work can be found in her Etsy shop, Rakstar Designs. Her writing can be found on her very dusty blog, The Pitter Patter Diaries (www.pitterpatterdiaries.com).

Allison McGinley lives with her husband and two children in suburban Philadelphia. When she's not dancing with her daughter or learning about Legos from her son, she writes, sings with a local worship band, and takes pictures of beautiful things. She shares her photography and reflections on Instagram at @allisonbenotafraid, and you can find her inspirational photography prints in her Etsy shop, "Be Not Afraid Prints."

Colleen Mitchell is a bringer-upper of boys, gospel adventurer, wanna-be saint, author, and speaker. She is the author of the award-winning *Who Does He Say You Are: Women Transformed by Christ in the Gospels*, and *When We Were Eve: Uncovering the Woman God Created You to Be*. Her latest adventure has taken her from the jungles of Costa Rica to the wilds of a sixth-grade classroom in Fort Wayne, Indiana, where she is still living her mission to give everyone she meets just a little Jesus.

Laurel Muff is a California girl who loves to travel, write, knit, read, and sing (but not necessarily in that order). She is married to her best friend and they have two beautiful girls together, whom she teaches at home. She loves to gather people around the table for delicious food and great conversation. With a heart for ministry, she is glad to share her faith in whatever capacity the Lord beckons her. She shares her musings on her blog: muffindome.com.

Heather Renshaw is a wife and mother of five living in the missionary territory of the Pacific Northwest. She loves deep conversation, loud singing, good eating, and silent Adoration. Heather is the author of an eight-week study on the Beatitudes, contribution author of *All Things Girl: Truth for Teens*, and is currently writing her first solo book for Catholic mothers called *Death By Minivan*. When she's not tackling the myriad tasks of her domestic church, Heather enjoys speaking at events, connecting via Twitter and Instagram (@RealCatholicMom), and dreaming big dreams. Heather may be found at www.RealCatholicMom.com

Kathryn Whitaker, a native Texan, is a wife and mom to six kids, teen to toddler. She shares her perspective on marriage, motherhood, college football, Texas BBQ, and her Catholic faith with honesty and authenticity on her blog, www.teamwhitaker.org. She's a frequent guest on Sirius XM's "The Jennifer Fulwiler Show" but all her kids really care about is what time dinner's ready. In her spare time, she operates her own graphic design business, working primarily with Catholic campus ministry programs around the country.

Kate Wicker is a Catholic wife, mom of five, recovering perfectionist, speaker, and the author of *Getting Past Perfect: How to Find Joy & Grace in the Messiness of Motherhood*, and *Weightless: Making Peace with Your Body*. When she's not playing the role of Uber driver, cook, or dispute resolution expert, Kate regularly contributes to myriad Catholic media. Her passion is encouraging women from all walks of life to reclaim the beauty of Creation and to recognize their worth. To learn more about her work and life, check our her highlight reel on Instagram (@KateWicker), or visit KateWicker.com

MEET THE ARTIST

Kristin Foss is the Art Director and Designer for Take Up & Read. She is a self-taught artist who focuses on bright hues and details. With a paintbrush in her hand and fresh cut foliage in a vase, she finds peace in God's word while putting brush to paper. Her studio is located in the countryside of Connecticut where she lives with her four children and husband. She enjoys painting, cooking, thrifting, and gardening. To follow her New England adventures, follow her on Instagram @kristin_foss

BIBLIOGRAPHY

The Bible. She Reads Truth Christian Standard Bible. Nashville: Holman Bible Publishers, 2017.

The Didache Bible: With Commentaries Based on the Catechism of the Catholic Church. San Francisco: Ignatius Press, 2015.

Dickens, Charles. *Bleak House*. London: Penguin Books, 2011.

Escrivá, Josemaría. *The Way of the Cross*. London: Scepter Publishers, 2004.

Hahn, Scott, general editor. *Catholic Bible Dictionary.* New York: Doubleday Religion, 2009.

Hahn, Scott, editor, and Curtis Mitch, compiler. *Ignatius Catholic Study Bible: New Testament*. San Francisco: Ignatius Press, 2010.

Lewis, C.S. *The Four Loves*. New York: Harcourt, 1960.

Trouvé, Marianne Lorraine. *The Sixteen Documents of Vatican II*. Boston, MA: Pauline Books & Media, 1999.

COLOPHON

This book was printed by CreateSpace, on 55# paper with an interior black and white.
Typefaces used include Brandon Grotesque, Essonnes, and Lora.
The cover is printed in full color with a soft touch matte, full laminate.
Finished size is 7" x 10".

Made in the USA
Las Vegas, NV
26 August 2022